SCIENCE CLUB

Steve Parker
and Raman Prinja

Sandy Creek
NEW YORK

Sandy Creek
NEW YORK

An Imprint of Sterling Publishing
387 Park Avenue South
New York, NY 10016

ISBN 978-1-4351-4413-2 (print format)

A CIP record for this book is available from the Library of Congress.

For information about custom editions, special sales, and premium and corporate purchases, please contact Sterling Special Sales at 800-805-5489 or specialsales@sterlingpublishing.com.

Manufactured in Guangdon, China
Lot #:
2 4 6 8 10 9 7 5 3 1
09/12

Created for QEB Publishing, Inc. by Tall Tree Ltd
Editors: Rob Colson and Jennifer Sanderson
Designers: Jonathan Vipond and Malcolm Parchment
Illustrations, activities: Lauren Taylor
Illustrations, cartoons: Bill Greenhead

Note

In preparation of this book, all due care has been exercised with regard to the activities and advice depicted. The publishers regret that they can accept no liability for any loss or injury sustained.

The practical activities in this book have been checked for health and safety by CLEAPSS, an organization that provides practical support and advice on health and safety in science and technology.

Words in **bold** are explained in the Glossary on page 115.

CONTENTS

FIZZING PHYSICS

AWESOME ASTRONOMY

BIOWORLD!

Living things are found on almost every part of our **planet**, from the bottom of the ocean to the highest mountain.

Living things range from germs that are too tiny to see, and bugs smaller than the dot on this "i," to huge blue whales. Some animals and plants are very common, while others live only in one specific place. Why not form a science club with your friends? You can explore your local area and discover the many living things that are all around you.

TINIEST BUGS

A magnifier or microscope makes small things look bigger and shows us a fascinating world of tiny creatures. This is the face of a minibeast called a tardigrade. About 20 of them would fit in this letter "o."

FASTEST HUMAN 27 MPH

FASTEST MOVERS

Nearly all animals move in some way. The fastest land animal is the cheetah. It races along at 68 miles per hour—almost three times faster than a sprinter.

SUPER TREES

Trees grow fast and tall in bright, warm sunshine. They are home to many animals who eat their leaves, flowers, and fruits, make nests in their branches, and dig tunnels among their roots underground.

IMAGINE THIS...
We can help animals, plants, and nature in many ways. One simple way is not to litter, which can injure wild animals and cause pollution.

BAMBOO FEAST
Many animals and plants are very rare and threatened by climate change and human activity. There are fewer than 3,000 giant pandas in just a few places in China. These creatures eat almost nothing but bamboo.

CHEETAH 68 MPH

GREEN AND GROWING

Seaweeds on the shore, soft mosses on a riverbank, tall conifer trees, beautiful flowers, rustling grass, bushes with delicious fruit, trees without leaves in winter —all these are plants.

Plants grow using sunlight. Their green leaves soak up sunlight and use the energy to make food such as sugars. To do this, they take in carbon dioxide, a gas from air, and give out another gas called oxygen. Most plants have leaves held up on a stem or stalk. Many plants lose their leaves and stop growing in winter. They start again when it is bright and warm in spring. Trees have thick, strong stems called trunks, made of wood. At the bottom are roots. These hold the plant in the soil, and take up water and mineral substances for it to grow.

EVERGREENS

Plants that keep their leaves all year long are called evergreens. Conifers, such as pines, and firs, make their seeds in woody cones.

SEAWEEDS

Seaweeds are a type of algae. They do not have proper roots because they have water and nutrients all around them. But many have root-like parts called holdfasts that attach them to rocks.

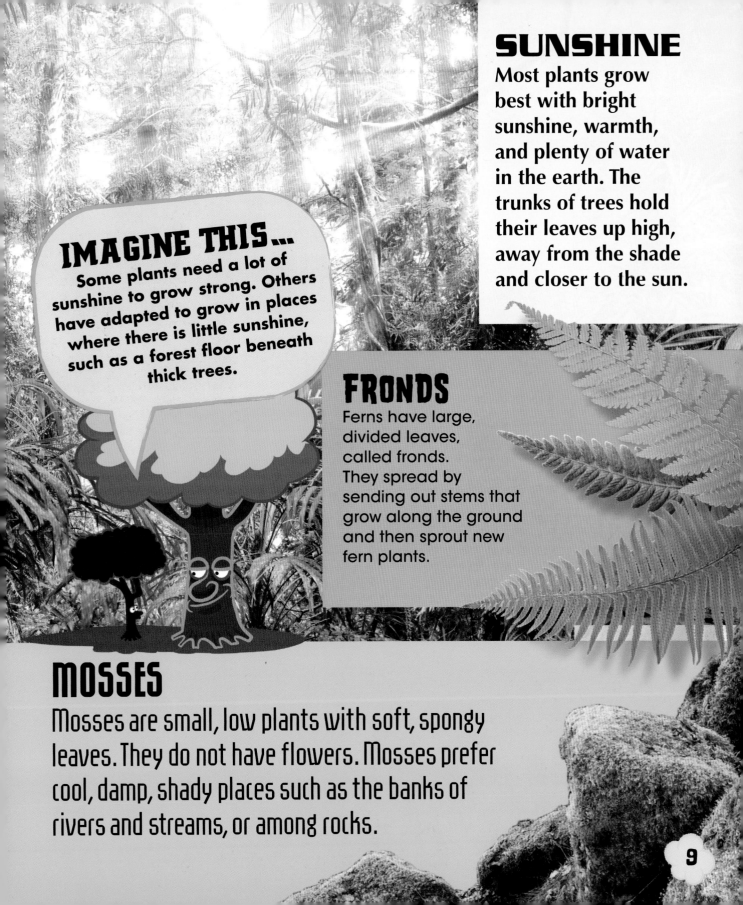

SUNSHINE

Most plants grow best with bright sunshine, warmth, and plenty of water in the earth. The trunks of trees hold their leaves up high, away from the shade and closer to the sun.

IMAGINE THIS...

Some plants need a lot of sunshine to grow strong. Others have adapted to grow in places where there is little sunshine, such as a forest floor beneath thick trees.

FRONDS

Ferns have large, divided leaves, called fronds. They spread by sending out stems that grow along the ground and then sprout new fern plants.

MOSSES

Mosses are small, low plants with soft, spongy leaves. They do not have flowers. Mosses prefer cool, damp, shady places such as the banks of rivers and streams, or among rocks.

FANCY FLOWERS, SUPER SEEDS

Plants do not grow flowers so we can admire their beautiful colors and lovely scents. Flowers are a plant's way of reproducing, or making more of its kind.

Most flowers have male and female parts. The male parts make tiny pollen grains. These must get to the female parts of flowers. This is known as **pollination**. Some pollen grains are blown by the wind, while others are carried by animals. When plants are pollinated, they can start making their seeds. When seeds find the right conditions, usually damp earth, they start to grow, or germinate, into young plants.

IMAGINE THIS...

Some plants and flowers look pretty but they can be dangerous. They might cause a skin rash or sneezing. Before touching unfamiliar plants, check with someone who knows if they are safe or not.

POLLEN CARRIER

Bees are common carriers of pollen grains. The grains stick to the bee's body and legs. Some bees also have special pollen "baskets" to carry the pollen. The bee also takes some pollen back to its home as food.

Pollen basket

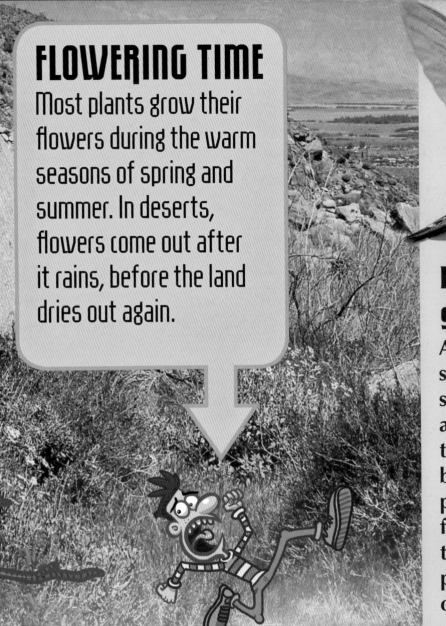

FLOWERING TIME

Most plants grow their flowers during the warm seasons of spring and summer. In deserts, flowers come out after it rains, before the land dries out again.

BRIGHT AND SCENTED

A flower's bright petals, its smell, or scent, and its sweet liquid, called nectar, all attract animals such as this hummingbird. As the bird feeds on nectar, pollen grains stick to its feathers. The bird then carries the pollen to other flowers.

NEW SHOOTS

When seeds land in the right conditions, they start to germinate. They make shoots, which grow leaves. Roots grow down into the earth, hold the plant in place, and take up water and nutrients.

GET GROWING

See how water can start a small seed growing into a whole plant, using food stored inside the seed.

1 Fill the bowl with water and add the beans. Leave overnight.

2 Press the paper towels against the jar sides. Add the sponges to the jar so that they press the paper towels against the sides of the jar.

3 Push several seeds about halfway down inside the jar between its sides and the paper towel, so you can see the seeds from the outside.

4 Pour about 1 inch of water into the bottom of the jar. Make sure it soaks into the paper towel so that the seeds are damp.

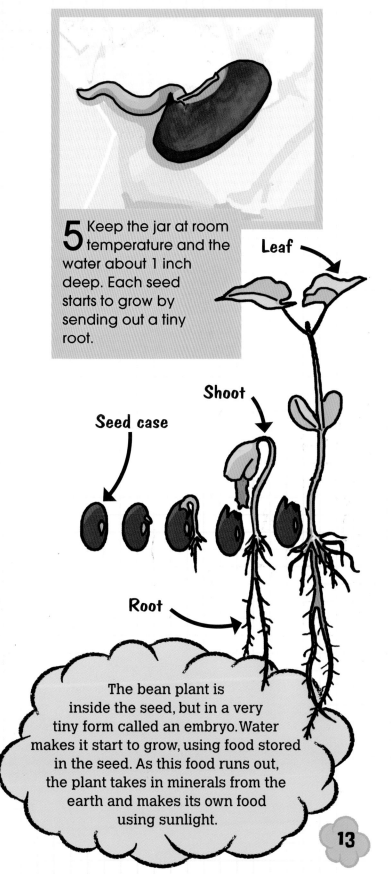

5 Keep the jar at room temperature and the water about 1 inch deep. Each seed starts to grow by sending out a tiny root.

Leaf

Shoot

Seed case

Root

6 Gradually, the root gets longer. Then, a green shoot grows out of the seed case. After a few days, the seed will run out of food, so ask an adult to plant it in a pot of earth. Keep watering and watch it grow!

The bean plant is inside the seed, but in a very tiny form called an embryo. Water makes it start to grow, using food stored in the seed. As this food runs out, the plant takes in minerals from the earth and makes its own food using sunlight.

13

LOOK AND LISTEN

Animals need to know what is around them, including food or enemies. They do this with their senses, such as seeing and hearing.

All kinds of animals have eyes to detect light. Animals that are out at night have extra-large eyes to detect as much light as possible. Ears are used to pick up sounds. The important hearing parts of the ears are inside the head. Birds have ears under their feathers. Reptiles, such as snakes, have ears that are thin patches of skin just behind the eye.

Snake ear

IMAGINE THIS...
Eyes are important but also very delicate. Make sure you protect yours, for example, by wearing sunglasses in bright sunlight.

BIG-EYED HUNTER
Owls have large eyes to see their victims from far away, even in the dark. Light goes into the eye through the dark-looking hole, called the pupil. After light enters the pupil, it hits the lens. The lens focuses light to make a clear picture.

INSECT EYES

The eyes of insects are like hundreds of tubes joined together. Each part sees just a tiny area, but all these areas join together for the whole wide view.

HEARING IN WATER

Fish have a stripe along each side of the body called the **lateral line**. This senses sounds, such as the clicks of a dolphin, and also ripples and movements nearby, such as the swish of a shark.

EXTRA-BIG EARS

The fennec fox's huge ears catch the tiniest sounds — even beetles or ants crawling across the ground. This is how the fox finds its food.

15

OPTICAL ILLUSIONS

Think you can trust what you see? Think again! Sometimes patterns and shapes can be arranged to trick your eyes and brain into seeing something that isn't actually there. This is called an optical illusion.

1 Hold the page upright and stare at the center of the spiral spokes. Slowly twist it left and right. Do the spokes twist?

2 Can you see gray spots flashing in the white circles? Now try to focus on just one of the spots. Does it disappear?

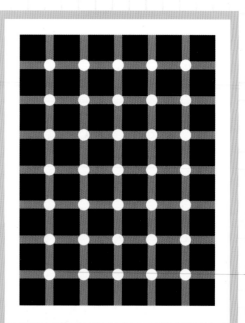

3 Your eyes can trick the way you see shapes! Look at the spaces between where the lines meet. Can you see circles?

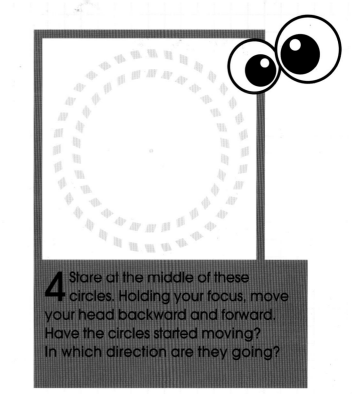

4 Stare at the middle of these circles. Holding your focus, move your head backward and forward. Have the circles started moving? In which direction are they going?

5 What do you see first when you look at this picture—a man playing the saxophone or the face of a woman? Can you see the other shape?

6 This illusion is all about lines. The red square looks like its sides are bending in. But its sides are actually straight.

ON THE MOVE

All animals move around during their life. Even creatures that seem to be stuck down, such as shellfish and sponges on the seashore, moved around before they settled on the rocks.

Birds and bats fly, fish and dolphins swim, and moles and earthworms burrow in earth. On land, some creatures walk and run, while others hop, jump, or slime along. Snakes have no legs, but they can slither quickly. In fish, reptiles, birds, and mammals, muscles pull the bones of the skeleton inside, to move the legs and other body parts. In creatures such as insects, spiders, and crabs, the muscles are inside the body casing and pull on the casing to move the legs, claws, and other body parts.

FLYING

Most insects, such as this Cockchafer (a European beetle), have wings and flap them to fly. The wings move down and back to push the insect up and forward. Some flies flap their wings more than 500 times each second!

RUNNING

Long legs are the sign of a fast runner, like this horse. The legs can cover lots of distance with each stride or step, pulled by muscles in its shoulders and hips.

SOARING

Some birds gain height without flapping by turning into the wind. This is known as soaring. A seabird, such as this albatross, can soar without flapping for days!

SWIMMING

Fish, such as eels, swim by bending their body from side to side. The body, fins, and tail push against the water and move the fish forward.

IMAGINE THIS...

Wild animals use their muscles to keep them fit. Humans are the same. Stay active, exercise, and keep your muscles healthy!

ATTACHED

Shellfish, such as these barnacles, begin their lives as small young, called larvae. They swim, float, and drift in the water until they find somewhere suitable to live. Then they stick down and stay there.

REFLEXES

Sometimes you make a sudden movement that you cannot control. This is called a reflex. It is an automatic action that you do not have to think about, usually to protect your body from harm.

YOU WILL NEED:

- flashlight
- mirror
- darkened room

2 Shine a flashlight on your face, but NOT directly into your eye. Watch the pupil. It should rapidly get smaller. After a minute, switch off the flashlight and watch. The pupil should gradually get bigger again.

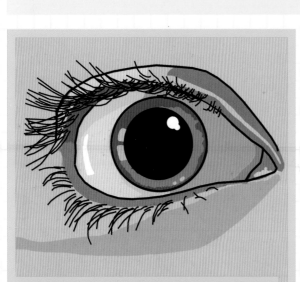

1 Spend a few minutes in a darkened room, then look in the mirror. Note the size of your pupil (the black hole in the middle of your eye).

The colored ring around the pupil is called the iris. In bright conditions, it makes the pupil smaller to prevent too much light damaging the eye. In dim conditions, it opens wider to let in more light.

REACTIONS

How fast are your reactions? And do they get faster with practice? A reaction is when you make a deliberate quick movement or action after something happens.

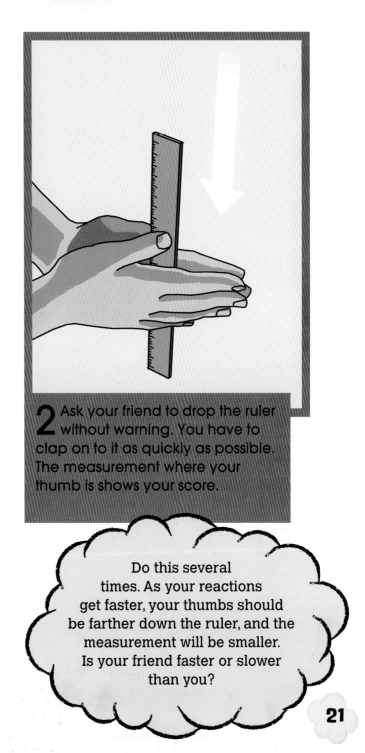

2 Ask your friend to drop the ruler without warning. You have to clap on to it as quickly as possible. The measurement where your thumb is shows your score.

1 Ask your friend to dangle the ruler with the zero-end down. Put your hands close together with your thumbs on either side of the ruler, level with the bottom of it, as if ready to clap.

Do this several times. As your reactions get faster, your thumbs should be farther down the ruler, and the measurement will be smaller. Is your friend faster or slower than you?

BITE AND SWALLOW

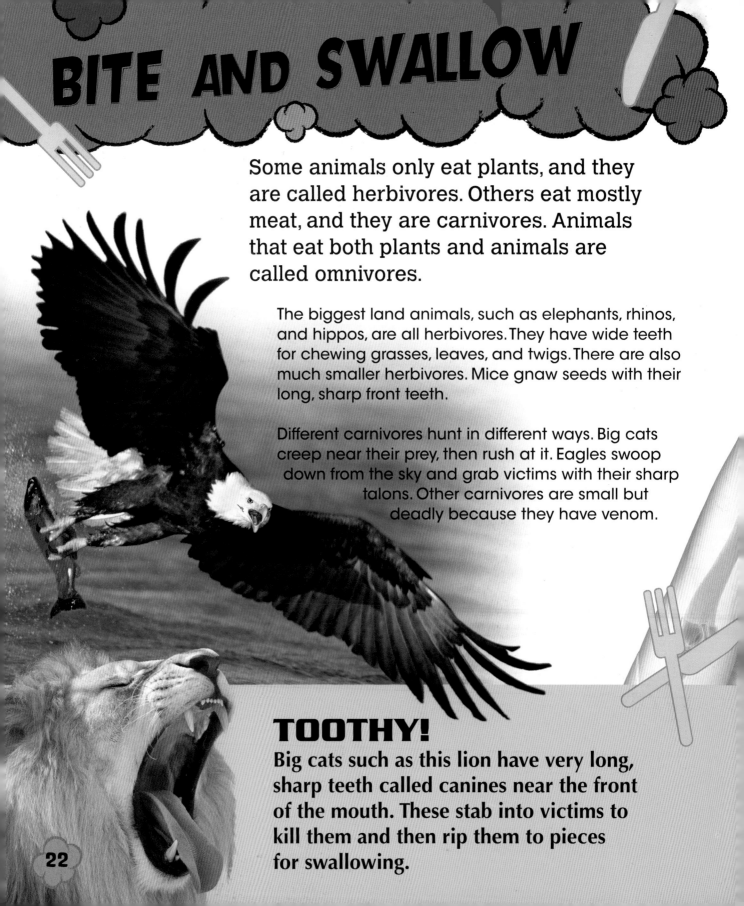

Some animals only eat plants, and they are called herbivores. Others eat mostly meat, and they are carnivores. Animals that eat both plants and animals are called omnivores.

The biggest land animals, such as elephants, rhinos, and hippos, are all herbivores. They have wide teeth for chewing grasses, leaves, and twigs. There are also much smaller herbivores. Mice gnaw seeds with their long, sharp front teeth.

Different carnivores hunt in different ways. Big cats creep near their prey, then rush at it. Eagles swoop down from the sky and grab victims with their sharp talons. Other carnivores are small but deadly because they have venom.

TOOTHY!

Big cats such as this lion have very long, sharp teeth called canines near the front of the mouth. These stab into victims to kill them and then rip them to pieces for swallowing.

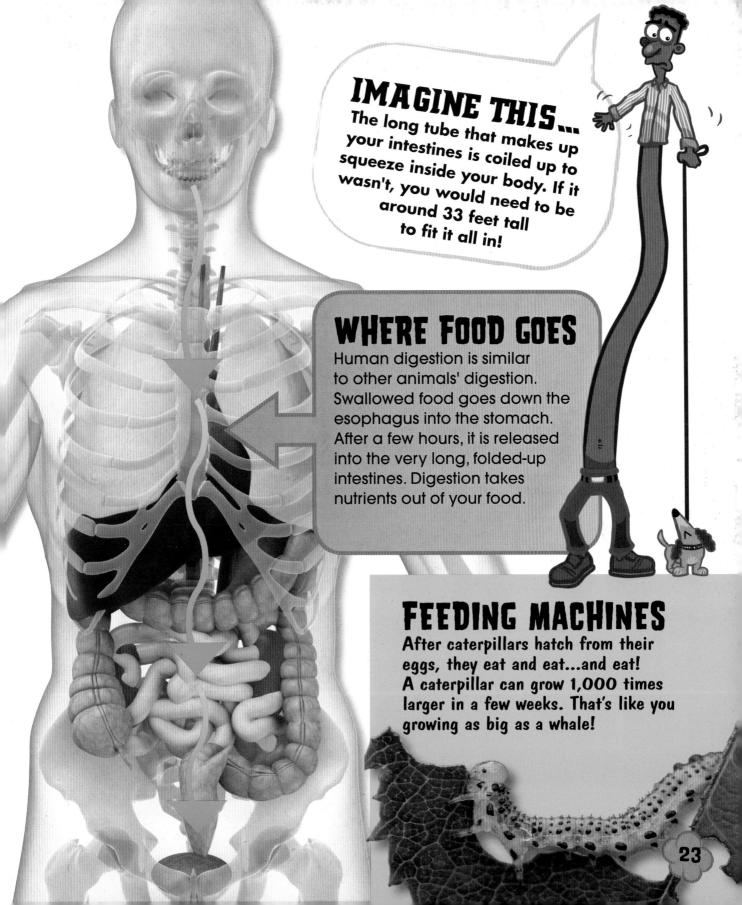

IMAGINE THIS...

The long tube that makes up your intestines is coiled up to squeeze inside your body. If it wasn't, you would need to be around 33 feet tall to fit it all in!

WHERE FOOD GOES

Human digestion is similar to other animals' digestion. Swallowed food goes down the esophagus into the stomach. After a few hours, it is released into the very long, folded-up intestines. Digestion takes nutrients out of your food.

FEEDING MACHINES

After caterpillars hatch from their eggs, they eat and eat...and eat! A caterpillar can grow 1,000 times larger in a few weeks. That's like you growing as big as a whale!

PANT AND PUMP

All animals need a gas called oxygen, which is in the air around us. They get it by breathing. Then the blood, pumped by the heart, spreads the oxygen and also nutrients around the body.

Mammals, birds, and reptiles breathe with two spongelike parts in the chest, called **lungs**. These suck in fresh air, take in the oxygen, and blow out the stale air. There is oxygen in water, too, where creatures breathe using parts called **gills**. A fish's gills are on the sides of its head, under flaps of skin. The heart is a strong pump, like a bag made of muscle. As it beats, it pushes blood around the body. All body parts need supplies of blood to bring them oxygen and high-energy nutrients, and to take away any waste.

BREATHING AND SOUNDS

Air coming out of the lungs can be used to make sounds by shaking, or **vibrating**, a part in the neck called the voice box (larynx). This is how people sing, dogs bark, and tigers roar.

BIG GILLS

Fish breathe as water flows in through the mouth, over the curved gills, and out through slits on the sides of the head. The gill slits on a basking shark are bigger than you!

24

INSIDE BLOOD

Blood contains millions of tiny parts called cells. Rounded red cells carry all-important oxygen. Pale white cells attack any germs that get into the body.

SEEING BLOOD

In some small creatures, such as this daphnia, you can see the blood and count the heartbeats. The hearts of small animals beat hundreds of times every minute. A blue whale's heart beats about 10 times a minute.

IMAGINE THIS...

Most creatures have one heart. But an octopus has three, and a worm has five! However, a worm's hearts are like thick tubes, rather than proper pumps.

FITNESS FUN

YOU WILL NEED:

- pen
- modeling clay
- drinking straw
- stopwatch
- notebook

When your body gets busy, running, or playing sports, your breathing and heart speed up. This sends more blood, with oxygen and nutrients, to your muscles. Count your heartbeats using your **pulse**. This is the throb of a blood vessel in your wrist that is caused by the surge of blood made by each heartbeat.

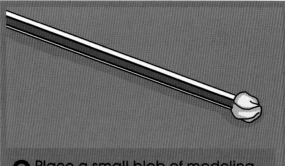

2 Place a small blob of modeling clay on one end of a straw. Press the blob onto your pulse mark so the straw is upright. The straw should move with each pulse, making it easier to count.

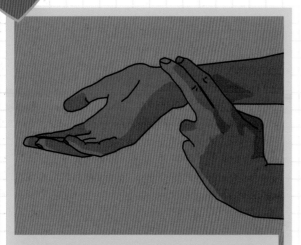

1 Feel your pulse in your wrist, using two fingers from the other hand. Put a small mark with the pen where it feels the strongest.

3 Sit still for five minutes. Measure and record your pulse over 15 seconds, then do the same with your breathing. Multiply these numbers by four to give your pulse and breathing rates per minute.

4 Take off the straw and jog in place for two minutes. This will make you breathe more rapidly. Sit down and put the straw back quickly. Measure your pulse and breathing as before. Repeat until both slow down to the resting rate again.

Draw a graph of the results, like those shown here. See how your breathing and heart speed up when you are active, then slowly return to their resting rates.

Pulse rate (Beats per minute)

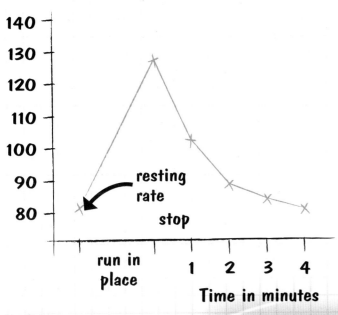

resting rate

stop

run in place

Time in minutes

Breathing rate (Breaths per minute)

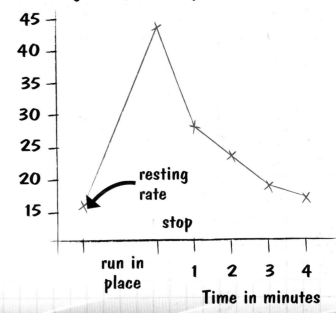

resting rate

stop

run in place

Time in minutes

GETTING FIT

Top athletes exercise every day to get in shape. This means that they can exercise for longer and will recover quickly after physical activity.

27

MAKING MORE ANIMALS

All living things make more of their kind—it is one of the main features of life. It is known as breeding, or reproduction. But different creatures do it in many ways.

Most animals lay eggs, usually in a place that is safe for the young when they hatch. Butterflies lay eggs on leaves so that the caterpillars are already on their food. Some creatures look after their eggs and also the babies. Birds keep their eggs warm, and feed and protect the baby chicks. Mammals such as whales and humans have babies rather than laying eggs. The mother mammal feeds her babies on her milk.

CHANGING SHAPE

Some creatures change shape a lot as they grow up. This is known as metamorphosis. A frog's eggs hatch into tadpoles with tails. Then the tadpole's legs appear, its tail shrinks, and it becomes a young frog.

frogspawn

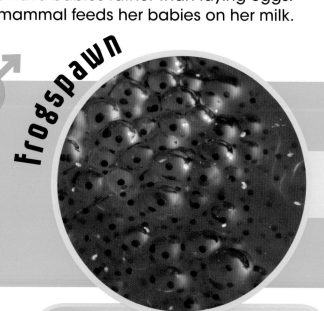

HATCHING

Baby crocodiles hatch from eggs, that have been kept warm in the earth or a pile of rotting plants. As soon as they emerge, they start to hunt small animals such as grubs and flies.

FAST GROWING

A young seal pup feeds on its mother's milk for about two weeks after it is born. The milk is rich in nutrients, so the pup grows fast. It is soon able to swim and feed on fish instead.

IMAGINE THIS...

A baby blue whale drinks 60 gallons of its mother's milk every single day! A human baby drinks only about ¼ gallons each day.

MILK

Tadpole

Frog

CARING FOR YOUNG

Bird parents spend so much time feeding their youngsters, they hardly have time for themselves. This bird will make over 200 feeding trips every day for its squawking chicks.

29

LOOK OUT, DANGER!

Wild places can be dangerous. Many animals and plants have special tricks and skills to defend themselves against enemies and stay alive.

Some creatures, such as snails, crabs, and shellfish, have hard shells to protect them. Prickly spines are used as defence by hedgehogs, sea urchins, and cactus plants. Another trick is to look like your surroundings so that enemies do not notice you. A young deer's spotted coat helps it hide in the undergrowth. This is known as camouflage. Some places get so cold in winter, that animals go into a long sleep, called hibernation. Other animals simply move away. This is called migration.

ARMOR

The armadillo has hard plates over its body to guard against **predators**, such as coyotes and cougars. It can dig fast and partly hide in a hole with just its hard back showing.

SPINES

A cactus does not have wide, flat leaves. Instead its leaves are long, sharp spines. These keep away plant-eating animals who want to munch on its juicy stem.

DEEP SLEEP

As winter approaches, the dormouse feeds hungrily and puts on weight as stores of body fat. These keep it going through its long winter sleep, in a nest among leaves and roots.

IMAGINE THIS...

The record for the longest migration is held by the Arctic tern. Every year it flies 24,855 miles between the far north and far south.

MIGRATION

When the dry season begins, plant-eaters like wildebeest and zebra start their migration. They walk hundreds of miles to places where rain has fallen and fresh plants have grown.

NOW YOU SEE ME...

See how camouflage works by making a really wild scene to test on your friends.

YOU WILL NEED:

- cardstock
- colored pens
- scissors

1 Draw a nature scene on a large piece of cardstock with dark brown trees, bright red flowers, vivid green grass, and blue sky.

3 Put them on the scene so one of each four is camouflaged on its own color and the others are on the other colors.

2 Draw small moth shapes on the card and color them in brown, red, blue, and green. Cut them out.

See how many moths your friend can spot in three seconds. If your friend was a hungry bird, he or she would notice the moths that were not camouflaged, and eat them first.

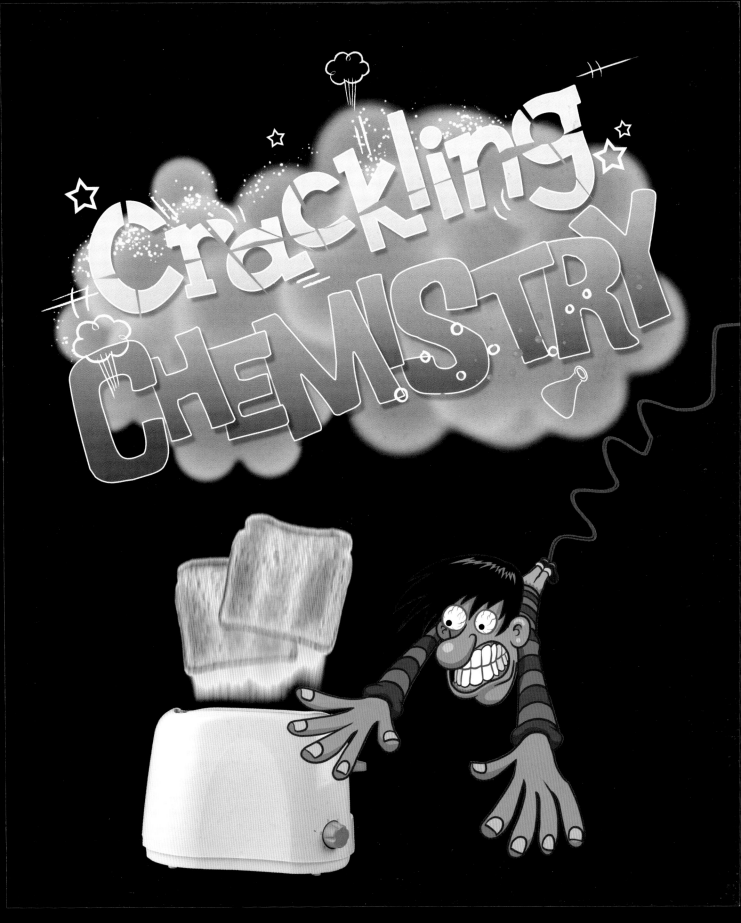

NOT MUCH USE!

What are these pages made of? Paper, of course. Paper is thin, light, **flexible**, and good for printing words and pictures. Paper is the right material, or substance, for the job. Imagine if these pages were made of bricks!

There are hundreds of different materials and substances all around you. Each one is designed for a certain use or task, and has certain features. It can be hard or soft, stiff or flexible, smooth or rough, and light or heavy. Materials are chosen for their different combinations of features.

IMAGINE THIS...

Some of the hardest materials are metals, such as iron and steel. They make sharp blades harder than the things they cut. A chocolate knife would be no good! Some metals are so hard they can be cut only with a powerful flame.

WHAT ABOUT ME?

Which materials do you use every day? Clothes are made from soft and warm fabric. Umbrellas need to stop the rain. They would not be any use if they were made from paper!

GET INVOLVED!

There are lots of activities and experiments in this book for you to try. Why not invite your friends over to help and start up your very own science club?

SHAPING

Statues and carvings are made from materials we can cut, shape, and polish easily, such as wood and stone. They can be cut and shaped using metal tools. Imagine carving a statue out of floppy jello!

GOOD AND BAD

Glass is good for windows. It lets light through so we can see what is on the other side. But glass has a problem, too. It is fragile and can break into very sharp pieces. We know we must be careful with it. The benefit of glass being seethrough is bigger than the problem of it breaking.

NATURAL OR NOT?

Can you make diamonds in an oven? Do plastic toys grow on trees? Some materials and substances are natural, or found in nature. Others are **artificial** and made by humans.

Substances that come from nature include many kinds of wood and stone, which we use for making furniture and houses. Artificial substances include plastics, some metals, glass, and pottery. They are produced from natural materials. We change these natural **raw materials** to make them hard, tough, and longlasting.

STRONGER THAN NATURE

Skyscrapers could not be built from natural materials alone. Stone is too heavy and wood is too weak. We need to use an artificial metal called steel to make the strong girders.

USEFUL FOR BUILDING

People have used wood and stone for building for thousands of years. Wood may rot and weaken, but stone can last forever. The Great Sphinx and pyramids of Ancient Egypt were built from stone around 4,500 years ago.

PRECIOUS MATERIALS

Precious gems and jewels such as diamonds and rubies are natural. They are found in rocks and then smoothed and polished so they sparkle. Other precious natural materials include metals, such as gold and silver.

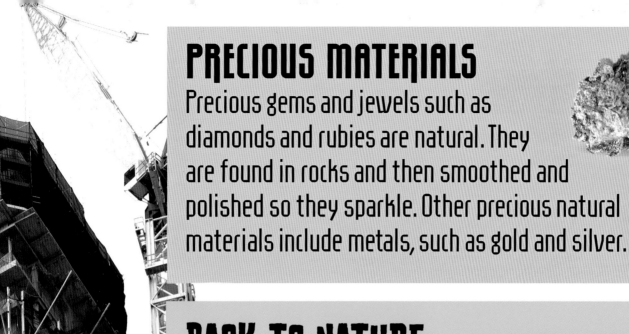

BACK TO NATURE

Many natural materials can be **recycled** by nature, but most artificial materials cannot. We must recycle them ourselves. You can recycle glass, some plastics, paper, and cans by sorting them and taking them to a recycling center.

IMAGINE THIS...

See how much of your everyday waste you can recycle. You might be surprised by how much garbage you can save.

Aluminum and steel cans

Newspapers, magazines, and cardboard packaging

Plastic bottles

Glass bottles

HARD AND SOFT

Soft, flexible materials are no use for building houses or bridges. And hard materials are useless for making clothes or sheets for your bed.

We make clothing, bedding, and similar products from natural materials such as cotton and wool. These contain millions of tiny, bendy, threadlike fibers that are woven or knitted together to create soft, bendable materials. Many kinds of metals are quite stiff or rigid, but they are also slightly flexible. They can bend a little rather than break.

NOT TOO LONG

Soft substances such as sponges and foams are made from elastic materials that bend and then spring back to their original shape. Bungee jump cords are made from very strong elastic material, such as tough rubber. The amount of stretch must be checked and measured often, to make sure they are safe and not weak or worn.

SHARK ATTACK?

Water is very heavy and it can push with great **force**. Big tanks or aquariums have glass sides that are extra-thick, so they do not crack under the pressure.

HARD

Diamond

Knife blade

Hardness is determined by how well an object scratches something. Harder objects scratch others more easily.

Copper coins

Pencil lead

SOFT

HANDLE WITH CARE

Some materials are very rigid—if you bend them too much, they will break. We say they are brittle. Glass and pottery will crack and snap into sharp pieces that are dangerous.

WOOL FOR US

Wool for fabrics is the long, soft hair or fur from sheep and other animals. About once each year, the wool is cut off or sheared, then it grows again. It doesn't hurt—it's like when you get a haircut.

39

STRONG AS... PAPER?

Different materials are suited to certain tasks. For example, paper is flexible and floppy. Or is it? The shape of an object can be as important as the material from which it is made. The challenge is to rest a book on top of upright sheets of paper.

YOU WILL NEED:

- medium-sized book
- about 16 sheets of paper (letter size is good)
- tape

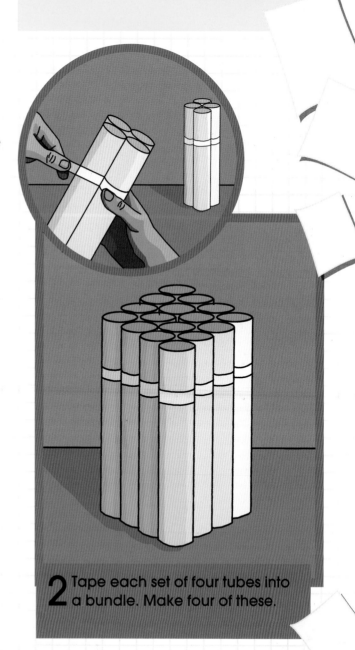

1 Try to stand the paper sheets on their ends. They cannot hold themselves up, let alone support a book. Roll each sheet of paper into a tube shape about 1¼ inches across and tape the ends together firmly.

2 Tape each set of four tubes into a bundle. Make four of these.

3 Place the tube bundles upright in a square or rectangle slightly smaller than the book. Lower the book gently, keeping it level. Now it should rest on the paper easily.

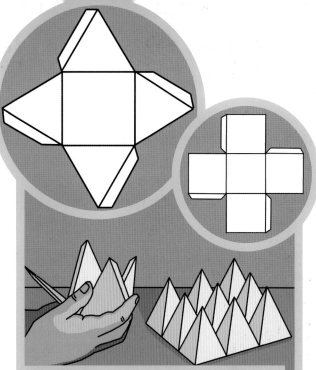

4 Use the patterns above to make pyramids or boxes instead of paper tubes. Do these hold the book up?

When the sheet of paper is flat, it is floppy and weak in all directions. If it is rolled into a tube, it becomes stiffer in one direction, end to end.

TOUGH TUBES

Look for places where tubes are used for strength. How about scaffolding, some types of girder bridges, and your bicycle frame?

ALL MIXED UP

Substances can get mixed up. Sometimes you can separate them, but other times substances seem to disappear, like sugar stirred into hot water. Where has the sugar gone?

A mixture is two or more substances blended together, which can be separated easily. But when sugar is added to water, it breaks up into pieces that are much too tiny to see. They spread out and float around in the water. This is called **dissolving**. A substance that dissolves is called the solute. What it dissolves in, for example water, is the solvent. Both together are the solution. There are other types of mixtures, such as suspensions and emulsions.

MIX IT UP

A suspension is a type of mixture where a solid substance is mixed with a liquid, usually by shaking or stirring them together. An emulsion is a special kind of mixture made up of two liquids that do not normally want to blend! They are mixed together by shaking and stirring, or by adding another substance to mix things up. Some wallpaints are emulsions. They are made of small drops of color that are spread throughout another liquid, such as water.

WHICH FLAVOR?

You can guess a drink flavor by the color of the substances dissolved in the water. Orange drinks are orange flavored. Red drinks might be raspberry or cherry, and pale green is usually lime flavor.

IMAGINE THIS...

Wash your hands often to remove dirt and germs. Cold water alone is no good. Warm water and soap dissolve dirt properly and get your hands clean.

SIEVING

Sieves are used to separate mixtures. They have a mesh of little holes. Items smaller than the holes pass through, but bigger ones do not. Sieves are used to separate grains of wheat from the rest of the plant.

WHAT A MIX-UP!

Oh no! The salt has accidentally spilled into the sand. How can you separate this mixture of tiny grains? You could use a microscope and a very thin pair of tweezers, but that would take a very long time. Dissolving and **filtering** are much easier.

YOU WILL NEED:

- cupful of clean sand
- cupful of table salt
- pitcher and bowl
- funnel with filter paper, paper tissues, or paper towels
- warm water

1 Mix the grains of sand with the grains, or crystals, of salt. Put the mixture in a pitcher or bowl.

2 Add the warm water to dissolve the salt, stirring well until all of the salt crystals have disappeared.

3 Pour the pitcher's contents through some filter paper or a similar material in a funnel into a bowl.

4 Allow the funnel, paper, and sand to dry. Then you can brush off the sand.

5 Leave the salt solution to dry in a warm place. The water will evaporate, which means it will turn into a gaslike vapor that mixes invisibly in the air. The salt will be left, probably as a crust. Stir this to get back to salt crystals or grains.

Dissolving—the salt grains dissolve in water. They become smaller and smaller until they are the tiniest particles of salt, known as molecules. These are much too minute to see as they float among the water molecules.

Filtering—the filter is like a net with tiny holes. Molecules of water and salt are so small that they easily pass through the holes. But grains of sand are much too big to pass through.

FREEZING AND MELTING!

When water becomes very cold, a strange thing happens. It turns rock-hard! We say it **freezes** into ice. As the ice warms, the opposite happens. It turns back into a liquid—it **melts** into water. Other substances can be liquid and solid, too.

Solids are usually hard and keep their shape. Liquids move or flow and take up the shapes of their containers. If liquids are heated they turn into gases. These can also flow and spread out to fill wherever they are. Whether a substance is solid, liquid, or gas is called its state.

ICICLES

In the cold of winter, dripping or falling water freezes into icicles. When the weather gets warmer, these melt back into a liquid state.

IMAGINE THIS...

Solid water, or ice, can be carved into amazing shapes. But it must stay frozen. Otherwise, the shape melts and drips away.

COLD

Air freezes -362°F

Water freezes 32°F

HEAT AND MELTING

Metals and plastics are solid—but not always. It depends on how hot they are. If you heat plastic, it turns soft and runny and becomes a liquid. The same happens to metals, but they need much more heat, usually until they are red-hot.

RED-HOT

Hot liquid metal, such as this steel, is poured into a shape called a mold. After the metal cools and hardens, it keeps its shape.

| Water boils | 212°F | | Gold melts | | Iron melts | 2,800°F | HOT |

COLDER THAN ICE

How can water be colder than ice? Try adding some salt to it and see what happens.

2 Put both cups in the freezer. Look at them every five minutes. Which one freezes first? Does the salty water freeze at all?

1 Fill each cup about two-thirds with water. Stir as much salt as possible into one cup.

When you add salt to water, it dissolves and its tiny molecules spread among the water molecules. As the solution cools, the salt molecules stop the water molecules joining together to form ice.

SAFE ROADS

In icy conditions, a mixture of grit and salt is spread onto roads. Salt makes it hard for water on the road to freeze. The grit helps vehicles' tires grip.

POWER OF ICE

Have you heard how water pipes freeze in cold weather, then leak when they warm again, causing a flood? This is due to the power of ice.

YOU WILL NEED:

- plastic cup with lid
- plastic bowl
- water
- freezer

1 Completely fill the cup with water and put on the lid so that there is no air inside.

3 The water expands, or gets bigger, as it cools, and then freezes with enough power to push off the lid.

2 Put the cup in a plastic bowl (in case of spills) and put it in the freezer for a few hours.

Most substances expand as they get hotter. Water expands as it freezes and pushes out with such force that it can break a pipe or container.

49

PHEW, BOILING!

Adding heat to a substance can change it from a solid into a liquid. But what happens if things get even hotter?

More and more heat can cause various changes. Most substances get bigger, or expand, as they get hotter. When a liquid gets hot enough, it boils and turns into a gas, or a vapor. The vapor contains the same tiny pieces as the liquid but these are much farther apart, so we cannot see them. They spread out and float away in the air. If the vapor then cools, it turns back into its liquid form. This is known as condensation.

BOILING HOT
When liquid water is heated enough, it turns into a gas called water vapor, or steam. Steam is useful for cleaning fabrics and is helpful in ironing creases out of clothes.

IMAGINE THIS...
Steam can also be used to make power. Hot rocks deep underground heat water, and this steamy water can be used to make electricity— and a nice, hot bath.

Lead boils 3,180°F

Mercury boils 674.4°F

Olive oil boils 572°F

Water boils 212°F

Ammonia boils -31.9°F

Hydrogen boils -423°F

BOILING POINT

The temperature at which a liquid turns into a gas is called its boiling point. Some substances, such as hydrogen, have a very low boiling point. Others, such as metals, have boiling points that are thousands of degrees.

COOL STUFF

When a gas cools enough, it turns back into a liquid. You can see this when steam touches a cool window and condenses back into liquid water.

SUBLIME STUFF

Some substances can change from a solid straight into a gas, without being a liquid. This is called sublimation. Dry ice is the solid form of carbon dioxide. It must be kept very cold. If it gets above –29.9°F it turns into a gas.

CARRY OR NOT?

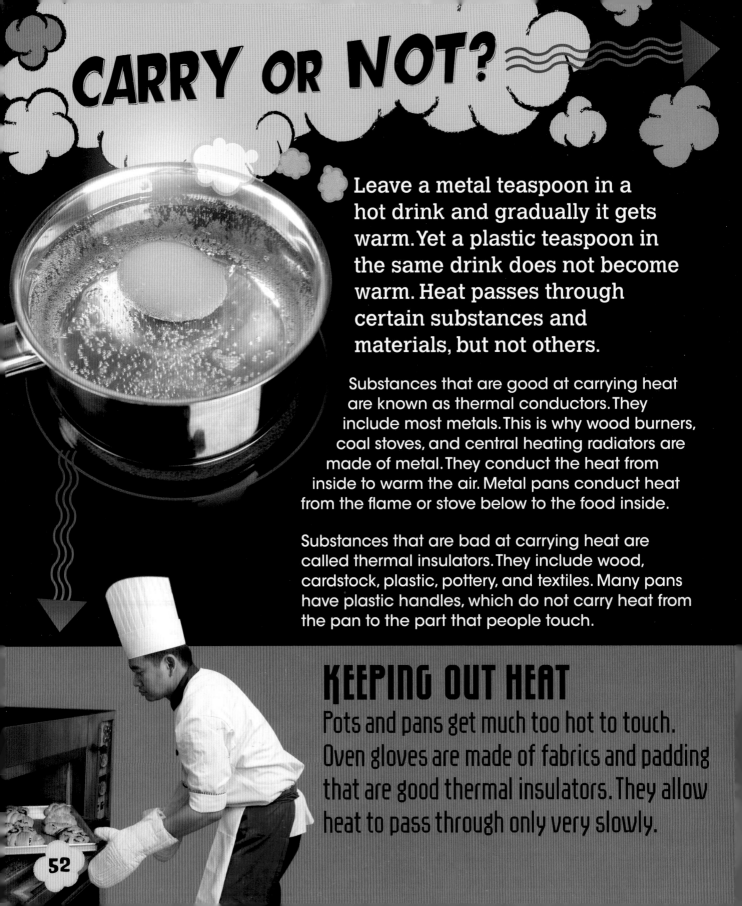

Leave a metal teaspoon in a hot drink and gradually it gets warm. Yet a plastic teaspoon in the same drink does not become warm. Heat passes through certain substances and materials, but not others.

Substances that are good at carrying heat are known as thermal conductors. They include most metals. This is why wood burners, coal stoves, and central heating radiators are made of metal. They conduct the heat from inside to warm the air. Metal pans conduct heat from the flame or stove below to the food inside.

Substances that are bad at carrying heat are called thermal insulators. They include wood, cardstock, plastic, pottery, and textiles. Many pans have plastic handles, which do not carry heat from the pan to the part that people touch.

KEEPING OUT HEAT

Pots and pans get much too hot to touch. Oven gloves are made of fabrics and padding that are good thermal insulators. They allow heat to pass through only very slowly.

KEEP IN THE HEAT

The home you live in is made from substances that are good at conducting heat. This picture shows how much heat is lost through different parts of a house. Keeping the roof and walls insulated and blocking drafts should keep you feeling cozy and your fuel bills low.

IMAGINE THIS...
Wearing the right clothes on a cold day will keep you warm—you wouldn't go skiing in just your bathing suit!

ROOF 25%

WINDOWS 10%

WALLS 35%

GAPS 15%

GROUND 15%

Space shuttle

HEAT SHIELD

When spacecraft return to Earth, they become very hot as they enter the **atmosphere**. To stop them from burning up, they are covered in special substances that do not conduct heat. The bottom of the space shuttle has thick tiles that create a heat shield.

53

CARRY THAT HEAT!

Which substances are good heat carriers, or conductors? Metals are good conductors, as this tasty test shows.

YOU WILL NEED:

- small lump of butter
- frozen peas
- long items such as metal spoon, metal kebab skewer, drinking straw, wooden or plastic chopstick, knitting needle
- pitcher of warm (not boiling) water
- adult help

1 Put the long items in the pitcher. Stick a pea to the top of each item with a small lump of butter.

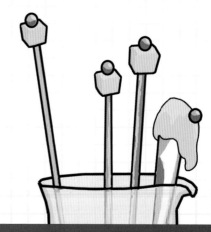

3 Which pea falls off first? The item it is stuck to is the best heat conductor. It carries heat from the water up to melt the butter. Which is the worst conductor or the best insulator?

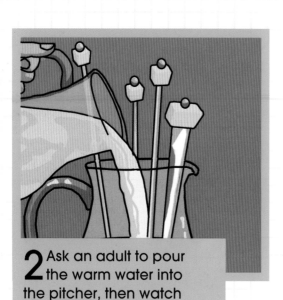

2 Ask an adult to pour the warm water into the pitcher, then watch and wait.

You could try this test using chocolate instead of butter. Chocolate needs more heat to melt, but it's tastier!

STOP THAT HEAT!

Which substances are good insulators and the worst conductors? Sometimes we want to stop heat moving around.

YOU WILL NEED:

- two plastic cups
- two ice cubes
- various materials such as cotton handkerchief, aluminum foil, bubble wrap, plastic wrap, paper towel
- thermos

1 Put an ice cube in each plastic cup and one in the thermos.

2 Wrap up the cups in the various materials. Leave one of the cups unwrapped.

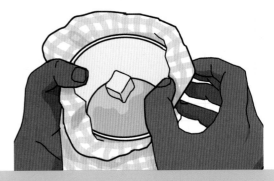

3 Every few minutes, check the cups and flask to see which ice cubes are melting and which are still frozen. Then wrap them again.

The materials around the cubes that stay frozen the longest are the best insulators. Does the cube in the thermos last the longest?

DON'T TOUCH!

"Danger! If this chemical touches the skin, wash it off at once with plenty of clean water, and seek medical advice!" Substances such as powerful chemicals need these health warnings.

Chemicals such as bleaches, oven cleaners, rust removers, insect killers, and drain clearers must be powerful in order to do their job. They cause chemical changes or reactions such as clearing blockages and dissolving dirt and grease. Some chemicals are strong acids, such as the hydrochloric acid in a car battery. They can damage substances by eating away at them. Other **corrosive** chemicals are alkalies, such as drain clearer. All of these powerful chemicals must be handled with care!

Chemical Labels

Dangerous chemicals usually have warning labels on them to tell people they're dangerous. Never put chemicals, liquids, powders, or similar substances into other containers, especially if they have the wrong label or no label at all.

IN THE FACTORY

Factory workers who use powerful chemicals are trained to understand the dangers, know about safety, and wear protective equipment. They should know what to do in case a chemical splashes or spills.

PESTICIDES

Pesticides kill damaging small creatures, such as caterpillars, worms, slugs, and grubs. But they may also harm people and pets. Farmers need to read the instructions and follow them carefully.

OUT OF REACH

In the home, powerful chemicals must be kept out of reach of young children who do not understand the dangers. In a locked cupboard or on a high shelf is a good place.

KITCHEN CHEMISTRY

School lessons teach us about different materials, heat and cold, freezing, melting, and boiling, mixtures, and changes. But what can you learn at home?

The kitchen is a great place to learn about chemical changes and physical processes. Soaps are used to dissolve dirt and grease off hands, dishes, and work surfaces. Ingredients are mixed in all sorts of combinations and can be heated in an oven or on a stove. Refrigerators and freezers keep food cold and help them stay fresher for longer.

CHANGING FOOD

By mixing different foods together, cooks can change what they look like, how they taste, and even how they behave. Jello is made by adding hot water to jello powder, pouring the runny liquid into a shape or mold, and then allowing it to cool. In hot weather, keep jello in the refrigerator or it will start to melt again.

ADDING HEAT

Heating foods can change them and make them good to eat. Boiling potatoes in water makes them soft, while broiling pieces of meat makes them tender and delicious. A kitchen may have several different ways of heating food. These include microwave and normal ovens, and stoves that have gas or electric burners to heat pans. Toasters have electric heating elements to warm bread to make toast.

KEEP IT COOL

Refrigerators keep food and drinks cool. This slows down the rate at which food goes bad and keeps it fresh for several days. Freezers are even colder. They can freeze liquids solid and stop food from going bad for weeks and even months.

IMAGINE THIS...

Refrigerators and freezers allow us to safely store and keep large amounts of food. Without them, we would have to eat all our food very quickly—or go shopping a lot.

59

ERUPTION!

Some chemicals react together to make new substances that are gases. You can see how this happens with a homemade erupting volcano!

YOU WILL NEED:

- tray
- plastic cup
- vinegar
- red food coloring
- baking soda
- sand or papier mâché

1 Put the cup on the tray. Fill the cup with vinegar. Add red food coloring for effect.

2 Make a volcano around the cup by building up sand or papier mâché in a cone shape.

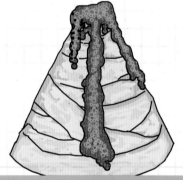

3 Add some of the baking soda into the vinegar, and watch what happens. The volcano bubbles and foams, just like a real one!

Vinegar contains the chemical acetic acid, and baking soda is sodium bicarbonate. When they mix, they cause a reaction that gives off the gas carbon dioxide, which makes the volcano "erupt."

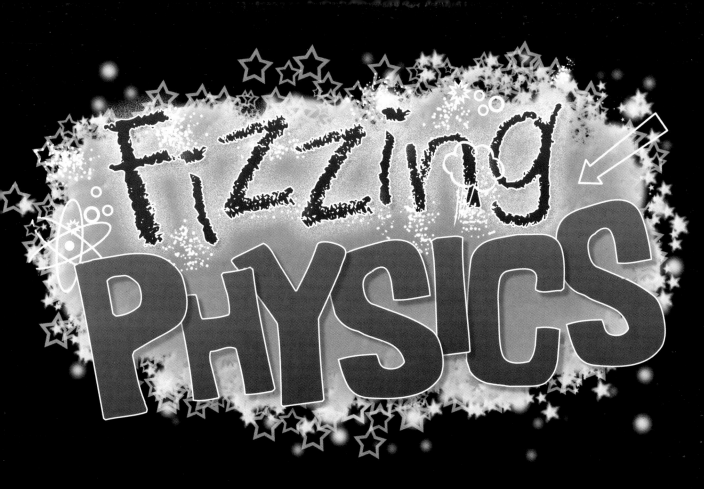

MACHINES EVERYWHERE

It is a hot day and you need an ice-cold drink. You have a bottle of soda, but its metal top is fixed on very hard. Using a bottle opener, you lever it off.

A bottle opener is a type of machine, called a lever. It lets you move something using a big force, but only a small way. Another simple machine is the wheel. You can roll a heavy load on it without too much effort. Ramps or steps are also simple machines. They let you move something upward in small, easy stages.

PLAY MACHINES

A playground has machines, not for work, but for fun. A seesaw is a lever and a merry-go-round is a type of wheel. There may be a pulley on a rope, too.

Simple Machines

The main simple machines are ramps, wedges (such as an ax blade), wheels and axles, screws (right), pulleys, gears, and levers. A ring-pull tab on a drinks can (left) is a lever. You can combine these simple machines to make more complicated ones. For example, a wheelbarrow (above) has levers for handles as well as a wheel.

REPAIRING MACHINES

When your bicycle breaks, you might use a simple machine to repair it. To tighten a nut, you need a wrench. This is a type of lever. It moves a nut a small distance, but with a great deal of force.

IMAGINE THIS...

Machines make jobs easier! Imagine what your life would be like if you did not have machines to help you.

WHEELS

The wheel is the ideal machine for rolling things along. You do not have to lift anything, you just push or pull. You can also use wheels on bicycles to zoom along quickly and easily.

GO AND STOP

IMAGINE THIS...
If something moves fast then suddenly stops, it can be damaged or harmed. This is why people wear seat belts in cars.

Many machines, from cars to jumbo jets, give you the force to keep moving. Their force comes from engines, but there are also natural forces that can move us, such as **gravity**.

Some forces, such as friction, or rubbing, make us slow down and stop. You can feel friction when you rub your finger against a rough surface—your finger will not slide easily over the rough surface. Friction can make things difficult to move. But it can be very helpful at keeping us in one place and in slowing us down.

FORCE OF GRAVITY

One force that works everywhere on the Earth is gravity. It pulls things downward. On a downward slope, such as a roller coaster track, gravity makes the roller coaster speed up.

LIFE-SAVING FRICTION

Without friction, climbers would fall off steep rocks. Climbers test each hand grip or foothold to make sure there is enough friction so that they can cling on.

SHOWING MOVEMENT

At an air display, the smoke trails from planes show how they move. They climb, turn, and go up and over and down in a circle, a move called looping the loop.

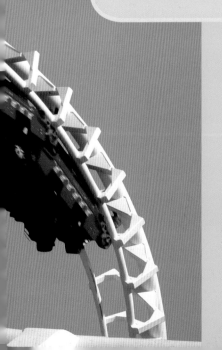

USEFUL FRICTION

Most of a motorcycle's working parts are smooth, hard, and well-oiled. But not the brakes! They press on the wheel brake disk to cause friction and make the motorcycle slow down.

ON THE SLIDE

Friction is the force that stops your plate sliding off your meal tray. Try this to see for yourself how friction works.

YOU WILL NEED:

- large plastic meal tray
- protractor
- small book
- old cell phone
- bar of soap
- pen
- piece of paper
- cooking oil
- roll of paper towels
- few dozen small marbles

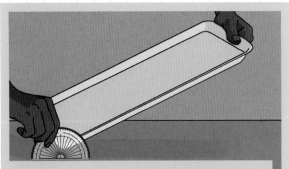

1 With the tray on a flat table, lift one end slightly. Practice measuring its angle with the protractor. A friend can help by looking at the angle from the front.

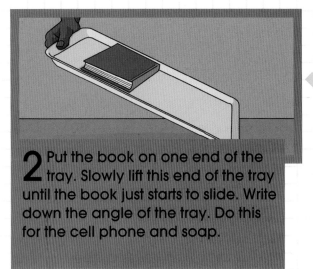

2 Put the book on one end of the tray. Slowly lift this end of the tray until the book just starts to slide. Write down the angle of the tray. Do this for the cell phone and soap.

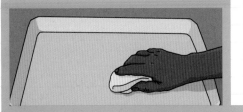

3 Put some cooking oil on some paper towel and smear the tray with the oil. Repeat step 2. The objects that stay on the tray at the highest angle have the most friction.

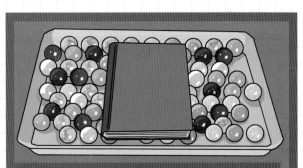

4 Clean the tray. Put the marbles on it. Balance the book on the marbles. How does this change the angle at which the book starts to slide? Are the marbles more effective than the oil at reducing friction?

Uneven surfaces

Layer of oil

Layer of oil reduces friction between the two rough surfaces

Every surface, even the smoothest, has tiny bumps and pits. The bigger these are, the more they rub and scrape past each other, and the greater the friction. Adding oil reduces the amount these bumps and pits rub together, and this lessens the friction.

SMOOTH RIDE
Objects roll more easily than they slide. Placing small balls between surfaces reduces friction because the balls roll rather than slide. Inside many machines, such as the wheels of a race car, metal balls, called bearings, are used to reduce friction and keep the machines working efficiently.

MUBADALA ABU DHABI

Santander

ETIHAD

Santan

LIGHT AND DARK

Darkness can be scary, especially if you do not know what is around you. Light is much better. Your eyes can see the shades, colors, and patterns that surround you.

Things that give out light are called light sources. For us on the Earth, the brightest light source is the Sun. Substances that let light rays go through them, such as glass, are called transparent. Substances that stop light passing through, such as wood, are called opaque. Light rays travel in straight lines and cannot curve around objects, so on the far side of an opaque object is a dark area known as shadow.

DAY AND NIGHT

Sunlight travels through space before it reaches us. As the Earth spins, the part of its surface facing the Sun has day, while the part facing away has night.

NEED FOR LIGHT

Many animals need bright light to see their surroundings. Tropical fish come from warm places where the Sun is usually bright and strong. They need a powerful light in their tank so that they feel at home.

IMAGINE THIS...
On really bright days, it is best to wear sunglasses and a peaked hat, or to stay in the shade. This way you will avoid glare and harm to your eyes.

SPOOKY SHADOWS

The dark shape behind an opaque object is called its shadow, or umbra. The shadow is the same shape as the object that is blocking the light. This can be a lot of fun when putting on a shadow puppet show!

MAKING LIGHT

When the Sun sets and it gets dark, we can make our own light by flicking on a light switch. Electricity flows through a light bulb, causing it to glow and give out light, turning darkness into light.

SEE THE LIGHT

You see light sources, such as an electric bulb, because they give out their own rays of light. These travel through the air and into our eyes. However, chairs, trees, people, and books do not give out their own light. So how do people see them?

Objects that are not light sources bounce back, or reflect, light that hits them. This is how you see them—by the light they reflect. If there is no light source, these objects would have no light to reflect, so we would not be able to see them.

MIRROR IMAGE

When you look in a mirror, you are seeing a reflection, which is a flipped image of yourself. If you raise your right arm, it looks like your image is raising its left arm.

REAR VIEW

Mirrors help you to see behind you. Race-car drivers wear helmets and are strapped in, so they cannot look over their shoulders. They have to use their rearview and side mirrors.

MOONSHINE

The **Moon** does not make its own light. You can see it because it reflects sunlight. As it goes around the Earth, the Moon appears to change shape as the amount of its sunlit part that we see on Earth changes.

IMAGINE THIS...

A flat, shiny surface produces a reflection. Curved or bent surfaces reflect the light rays in a different way, so the image is an odd shape—which can be funny.

STILL WATER

The surface of still water is like a smooth mirror that reflects light from the scene into our eyes.

COLORS GALORE

Most people like rainbows, but where do they come from? Ordinary white light from the Sun, a lamp, or a flashlight is made of a mixture of all the colors of the rainbow. These are called the spectrum. Follow these steps to see them.

As white light travels from one substance to another, such as from the air into a glass **prism** or a raindrop, it bends, or refracts. Each color refracts by a slightly different amount, so the colors separate to form a spectrum.

1 Next time it is both sunny and raining, look for a rainbow. Rainbows are formed by raindrops scattering rays of light.

2 Look at a DVD's blank side near a bright lamp. Twist and turn the DVD until you see a spectrum. You can probably angle it to see more than one spectrum!

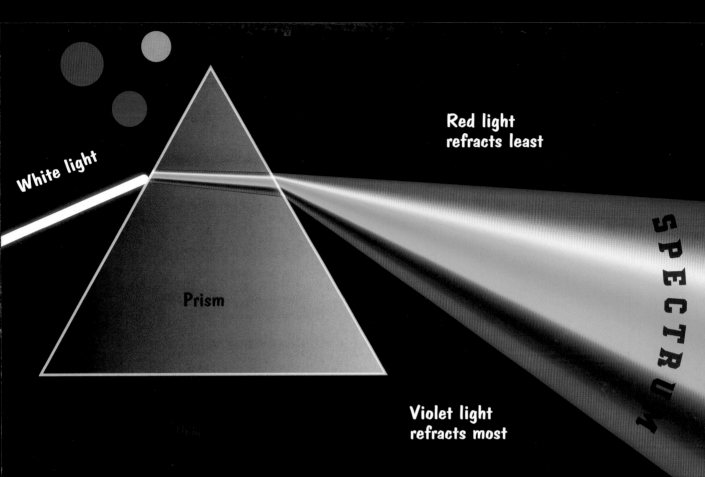

White light

Prism

Red light
refracts least

Violet light
refracts most

SPECTRUM

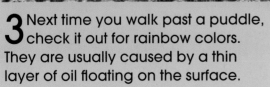

3 Next time you walk past a puddle, check it out for rainbow colors. They are usually caused by a thin layer of oil floating on the surface.

4 In a dark room, shine a flashlight through a clear glass of water onto some black cardstock. Angle the beam of light to produce rainbow colors on the cardstock.

STOP THAT NOISE!

People sometimes say: "It is so noisy, I can hardly hear myself think!" Loud noises can confuse people, while other sounds can be pleasant and relaxing.

Sounds travel through the air as sound waves. A sound comes from a source such as headphones, a television, an engine, and your own voice. A sound source must shake back and forth quickly, known as vibrating, to make its waves.

Sounds that we like and enjoy can be made by musical instruments or birds or people singing. Noisy sounds, such as traffic or jet planes roaring past, dogs barking, vacuum cleaners, and fire or burglar alarms are unpleasant. We usually want them to stop.

ANNOYING SOUNDS

Some sounds can be unpleasant. Loud, harsh sounds, such as noisy traffic, make us screw up our faces and put our hands over our ears to keep them out. After a while, they put us in a bad mood.

MAKING MUSIC

Some sounds, such as those from the instruments in an orchestra, go well together. All kinds of objects can be used to make musical sounds, from hoses to trash cans!

ANIMAL SOUNDS

Animals use sounds to send messages. Dog barks can mean "Beware!" A bird's song can be used to show off its lovely voice. Frog croaks and grasshopper chirps can often say "Let's play!"

Frogs croak to attract mates

HUMAN SOUNDS

Everyone can be a sound source in a number of ways. You talk, shout, and sing using the voice box in your neck. You can use other body parts to make sounds. You can clap your hands and stamp your feet, and even whistle.

VIBRATE

Something must vibrate to produce a sound. This can be the vocal cords inside your voice box or a string on a guitar. As it vibrates, it squeezes and stretches the air next to it, starting sound waves that move out.

IMAGINE THIS...

Male Humpback whales sing long and beautiful songs to attract female humpbacks. Their songs can be heard by other whales hundreds of miles away.

75

FAST, HIGH, AND LOUD

SOUNDS FAST!

Sound waves move through the air at about 1,115 feet per second. When jet fighters roar through the air faster than the speed of sound, they are called supersonic.

Sound waves travel through the air like waves traveling through a slinky (below), squashing and then stretching the air in succession.

The loudness of a sound is called its volume. If the radio is too quiet, you turn it up using the volume control. Whether a sound is high or low is called its pitch. This can range from the high cheep of a bird to the deep boom of thunder.

Wavelength

HIGH AND LOW

The pitch of a sound depends on the wavelength—this is the distance between each sound wave. The shorter the wavelength, the higher the sound.

Whisper
20dB

TOO HIGH FOR US

Noises that are too high-pitched for us to hear are called ultrasound. Bats find their way by making ultrasonic squeaks and listening to the echoes that bounce off objects.

Loud shout 80-90 dB

Chainsaw
100-110 dB

Bomb exploding
200 dB

QUIET AND LOUD
The loudness or volume of a sound is measured in decibels (dB).

BOTTLE PANPIPES

You can make your own musical instruments from throw-away or recycled items around the house. Make your own panpipes and blow your audience away with a good tune.

YOU WILL NEED:
- several identical drinks bottles
- pitchers of water

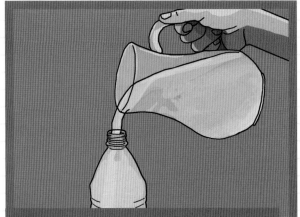

2 Put some water in one bottle and see how it changes the sound, making it higher in pitch. You may have to change how hard you blow.

1 Put the bottles in a row next to each other on a table. Blow across the top of one of them to make a hooting sound.

3 Put increasing amounts of water in the bottles along the row. In each bottle, there is less air to shake, or vibrate, so the note is higher.

4 If you have a guitar or piano, adjust the water to "tune" the bottles. Now you are ready to play!

BUCKET DRUM

YOU WILL NEED:

- empty food and drink cans of different sizes
- two large spoons
- old bucket (metal is best)
- tape

Once you've made the bottle panpipes, you can build a drum kit and form your very own junkyard band.

1 Tap each can with a spoon to hear the pitch of the sound it makes. Put them in order from lowest to highest pitch.

2 Turn the bucket upside-down. Tape the cans in order around the bottom of the bucket, level with the bottom of the bucket.

3 Using your spoons as drumsticks, beat out the main rhythm on the bucket and add in faster taps on the cans.

You could make a "guitar" with a shoebox and rubber bands. You could also tap a row of glass jars or bottles with different amounts of water in them to make a xylophone.

79

THAT'S ELECTRIC!

Electricity powers our modern world. It can be sent long distances along wires and it can be used in many ways, from lights to motors, radiators, and sound equipment.

Only some substances carry electricity. They are known as electrical conductors. Most of these are metals. Copper and silver are especially good conductors. Water is also a good conductor. Substances that do not carry electricity are called electrical insulators. They include wood, plastic, cardboard, fabrics, and pottery or ceramics.

IMAGINE THIS...

Batteries might be handy and portable, but make sure that you use the right batteries for each appliance.

POWER PLANTS

Electricity is made in power plants. Some power plants burn fuel such as coal, oil, or gas. This turns water into steam, which spins turbines to generate the electricity. Wind farms (above) use wind to spin turbines.

DANGER!

Wires, cables or power lines on big towers and pylons, and machinery such as transformers, all carry very strong electricity. You should never mess around with these, or with the plug sockets in your home.

HOW MUCH?

The strength of electricity is measured in volts (v). Voltages range from very low-powered batteries to very high levels in overhead power cables.

PORTABLE POWER

Batteries make electricity from chemicals. They power small moveable gadgets, such as toys, cell phones, music players, and flashlights. They can also be used to power large devices, including cars, such as this Tesla Roadster. Instead of using gasoline, you plug a battery-powered car in to recharge before zooming off again.

Tesla Roadster

HIGH

Grid
400,000 volts

Household power
220-240 volts

Batteries
1.5-12 volts

LOW

POTATO POWER

Batteries make electricity from the combination of chemicals inside them. You can do the same using a potato!

YOU WILL NEED:

- two big fresh potatoes
- two short pieces of thick copper wire
- two **galvanized** nails
- six crocodile clips
- insulated wire
- light-emitting diode (LED)

2 Using the clips and insulated wire, connect the nail in potato 1 to the copper wire in potato 2.

1 Number the potatoes 1 and 2. Push a nail into each potato, most of the way down. Insert a piece of copper wire into each potato, as far away from the nail as possible.

3 Again using the clips and insulated wire, connect the copper wire in potato 1 to one contact on the LED.

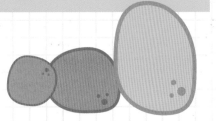

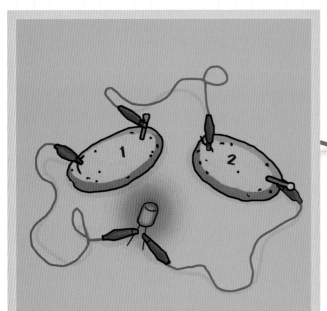

Potatoes contain chemical energy. In the potato battery, the zinc on the galvanized nail, the chemicals in the potato, and the copper in the thick wire, all react together to make an electric current.

4 Finally, connect the nail in potato 2 to the other contact on the LED. When you do this, you make a complete circuit, and electricity starts to flow. The electricity will make the LED glow.

Add more potatoes with their nails and copper wires to the circuit. Make sure you connect the nail of one to the copper wire of the next. Does the bulb glow brighter? Try fruits such as cucumbers, tomatoes, apples, and bananas. Which one works best?

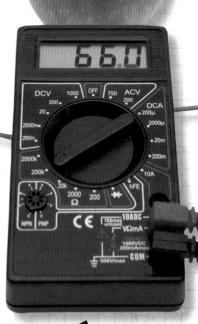

This device can measure the electric current of different objects— including fruit!

MYSTERY MAGNETS

One of the strangest forces cannot be seen, but can push or pull with huge power. This mysterious force is magnetism, and it is used in hundreds of machines.

Magnetism particularly affects iron objects. Steel is mostly iron, and is used to make many items, from silverware to refrigerators. Magnets stick to these objects. A magnet has two poles where its force is strongest: one pole is North (N) and the other is South (S). When two magnets come close together, if their poles are "like" or the same, they push apart, or repel. Two different or "unlike" poles pull together, or attract.

FLOATING MAGNETS

Some trains use magnets to zoom along. A magnet underneath the train pushes against a magnet on the tracks with so much magnetic force that the train actually floats! This type of train is called a maglev train, which is short for "magnetic levitation" (lifting).

MAGNETIC FIELD

The force of a magnet acts in an area called the magnetic field. The field curves around between the poles of the magnet. You can see this by scattering iron filings around a magnet. The iron filings will line up in the pattern of the magnetic field.

MAGNETS AND INFORMATION

Information is stored on computer hard disks as patterns of tiny magnetic spots. A hard disk is usually a stack of metal circles, each with a very thin magnetic coating.

IMAGINE THIS...

The main law of magnetism is like poles repel and unlike poles attract. So...

N + N = REPEL
S + S = REPEL
N + S = ATTRACT

COOL MAGNETS

Small, button-shaped magnets with plastic covers can hold notes to a steel refrigerator casing. The magnetism passes through thin paper, but is much weaker with thicker paper or card.

MAGNETIC FISHING

You can discover which substances are magnetic and try your hand at fishing at the same time!

YOU WILL NEED:

- string
- wooden spoon
- strong magnet
- pencil
- cardstock
- scissors
- tape
- variety of small objects

2 Draw and cut out fish-shaped cardstock. Tape a small object to each fish.

1 Tie string to the end of the spoon and around the magnet to make a "fishing rod."

3 Go fishing! Try to pick up each fish one by one with the magnet. Which objects stick to it best?

Substances that contain iron, such as steel, are attracted to magnets. Paper clips, nails, and bolts should work well. Thumb tacks and metal fasteners may work—but they could be made of other metals.

Awesome ASTRONOMY

WHAT IS ASTRONOMY?

Astronomy is one of the oldest branches of science. It is the science of space beyond the Earth. Astronomy is the study of the planets, moons, stars, **galaxies**, and all the other objects in the **universe**.

Scientists who study objects in space are called astronomers. They explore the universe using telescopes and computers to reveal amazing objects, including exploding stars (such as the stunning Crab Nebula, right), crashing galaxies, and **black holes** that trap light. But astronomy is also a science that can be enjoyed by anyone standing outside and looking up at a clear night sky.

HIGH TECH

Astronomers use powerful telescopes to look at the sky. Some of the telescopes are perched on mountain peaks, far away from the glare of streetlights and cities.

IMAGINE THIS...

Look up at the starry night and think of all the objects up there. Perhaps there are other forms of life somewhere. You could start your own astronomy club with friends and star gaze together!

WAY BACK IN TIME

Astronomy has been of great importance ever since ancient times. The movements of the Sun, Moon, and stars were used to make calendars by the early Babylonian, Chinese, and Egyptian civilizations. Sailors of the past were guided across the seas by charting the stars. Many ancient monuments, such as Stonehenge in the UK (below), were built to represent the positions of objects in the sky.

ROCKS, GIANTS, AND DWARFS

The Earth belongs to a family or system of planets that all **orbit** the Sun. The Sun itself is a star, like many of the other faraway stars you can see on a clear night in the sky.

Our **solar system** is made up of the Sun, eight planets, many moons, and many dwarf planets. Lots of smaller bodies, such as **asteroids** and **comets**, also travel around the Sun.

JUGGLING NINJAS!

In order away from the Sun, the planets are Mercury, Venus, Earth, Mars, Jupiter, Saturn, Uranus, and Neptune. To remember these names in the right order, try the sentence below:

"My Very Excited Monkey Juggled Seven Ugly Ninjas"

Use the first letter of each word for the right planet.

Sun

Mercury

Venus

Earth

Mars

Light from the Sun takes eight minutes to reach the Earth

ROCKY WORLDS

The four closest planets to the Sun are rocky worlds. The Earth is the only planet with liquid water on its surface. This water has made life on Earth possible.

WHAT'S UP WITH PLUTO?

Pluto was once known as a planet, but it is now known as a dwarf planet. Astronomers think there may be more than 50 bodies in the solar system that are just like Pluto. These objects are different from the eight planets because they are very small and their paths around the Sun are not always clear of other bodies.

A FRUITY SOLAR SYSTEM

Imagine we made everything about a billion times smaller. The Earth and Venus would be the size of a grape, Jupiter a grapefruit, and Saturn an orange. Uranus and Neptune would be a pair of lemons.

Saturn

Uranus

Neptune

Jupiter

GAS GIANTS

Jupiter, Saturn, Uranus, and Neptune are known as gas giant planets. They are very large and mostly made of hydrogen and helium gas.

91

OUR STAR, THE SUN

The Sun is the largest body in the solar system. Almost 99 percent of all the mass of the solar system is contained in the Sun. The Sun is a huge, hot ball of glowing gases.

The Sun is really a small-sized star, and there are many similar stars in the night sky. The Sun looks much bigger and brighter from the Earth because it is much closer to us than the rest of the stars. The next nearest star to us, Proxima Centauri, is almost 270,000 times farther away. If the Sun were reduced to the size of a basketball and placed in London, Proxima Centauri would be a smaller ball somewhere in California.

Convective zone carries energy to the Sun's surface

Energy passes through radiative zone

MOODY SUN

The Sun goes through times when it is either steady or very active. This cycle in its behavior happens every 11 years. When the Sun is at its most active, many features can be seen on its surface. Sometimes there are dark spots known as sunspots. The Sun can also release huge amounts of gas and particles in an explosion known as a flare.

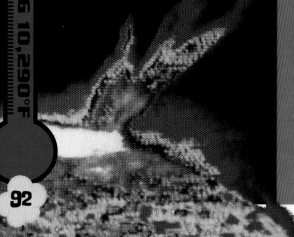

AURORAE

The Sun's flares send electrically charged material into the Earth's atmosphere, creating beautiful light shows near the North and South Poles. These are known as aurorae (or the northern and southern lights).

Core produces energy

SUPERPOWER

The Sun is made up of several different layers. Its incredible energy is produced in its center, or core. Here, a process called nuclear fusion takes place, and the gas hydrogen is turned into another element called helium. During this process, the Sun produces an enormous amount of energy. We can use some of this energy on the Earth using solar panels (below).

IMAGINE THIS...

You cannot visit the Sun. The main reason is that it is very hot. Even if you could get close, there is nowhere to land since it is a giant ball of burning gases!

PLANETS ON STRINGS

The giant gas planets (Jupiter, Saturn, Uranus, and Neptune) are much larger than the four rocky planets (Mercury, Venus, Earth, and Mars). Make this solar system mobile and hang it up to see how the planets size up.

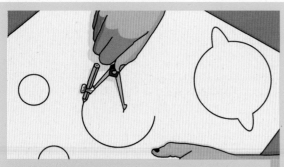

1 Using compasses, draw and cut out a circle for each of the eight planets from the white cardstock. Use the following diameters:

Mercury	¼ inch
Venus	⅔ inch
Earth	⅔ inch
Mars	½ inch
Jupiter	6½ inches
Saturn	5½ inches
Uranus	2¼ inches
Neptune	2 inches

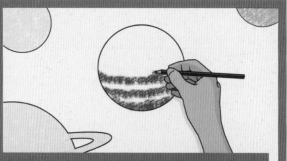

2 Color in both sides of the circles. Use gray for Mercury; yellow or orange for Venus; blue, white, green, and brown for Earth; reddish-orange for Mars; red or brown with white stripes for Jupiter; pale yellow for Saturn; light blue for Uranus; and blue for Neptune.

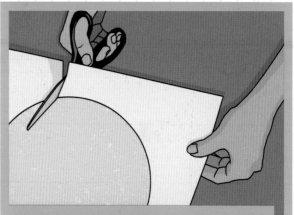

3 The Sun is too big to show on the same scale as the planets. Instead, draw and cut out a circle 8 in. in diameter. Color it yellow on both sides.

94

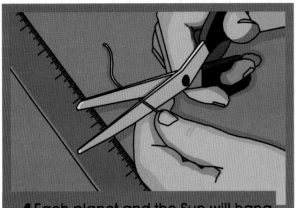

4 Each planet and the Sun will hang from the paper plate by string. Cut pieces of string the following lengths: 6 in for Mercury, Venus, Earth, and Mars; 8 in for the four giant planets; and 4 in for the Sun.

5 Attach each piece of string to the corresponding planet. Tape the strings to the plate. The Sun should be in the center with Mercury, Venus, Earth, and Mars forming an inner circle around it. The outer planets should be on a bigger circle close to the plate's edge.

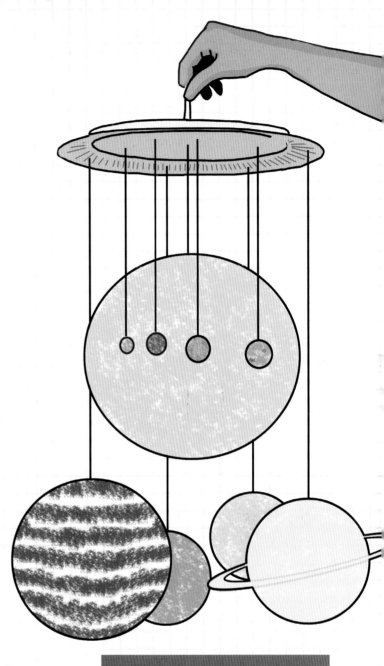

6 Cut another piece of string and tape it to the middle of the other side of the plate. Make a loop on this string so that your solar system mobile can be hung up.

THE EARTH AND ITS MOON

the Moon is 239,000 miles from the Earth

The Earth and its Moon make a very special pair in the solar system. Our home planet, the Earth, is the only one known to support life. The Moon is a very different place—cold and dry.

Our planet has an atmosphere of mainly nitrogen and oxygen gas, and liquid water on its surface, which make life possible. Our Moon is a cold, dry, and dead object. Its surface is covered in many **craters**, rocks, and a fine dark gray dust. There is no air to breathe on the Moon, nor is there water to drink.

ACTIVE

The Earth is one of the most active planets. There are regular earthquakes caused by movements of its crust and volcanic eruptions from beneath the crust.

A MONTH

The word "month" comes from the word for "moon" in old English. The Moon orbits the Earth once every 27 days. That is nearly one month for each orbit.

MOON DRAWINGS

Looking at the bright circle of the Moon at night, you can see dark and light patches on it. It is almost as if someone has been drawing pictures on its surface. What pictures can you make out from the light and dark patches? Some people say they can see a rabbit, while others imagine a lady reading a book. The dark and light patches are really different types of surface on the Moon. The dark areas are smoother land where lava from volcanoes flowed billions of years ago. The lighter areas are high mountains.

MOON WALK

Only 12 people have ever walked on the Moon. An airplane cannot fly there, but if it could, a jumbo jet would take nearly 20 days to reach it! In the late 1960s and early 1970s, the Apollo space rockets used by the National Aeronautics and Space Administration (NASA) flew astronauts to the Moon in just four days. When you get there, walking on the Moon would be like striding across a trampoline, because the Moon has weaker gravity than the Earth.

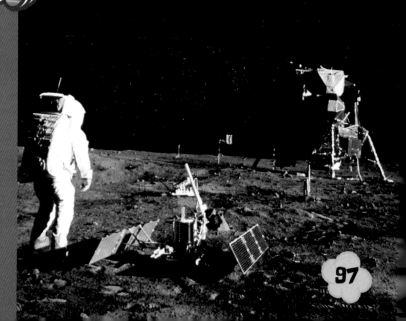

97

CRATERS IN A TRAY

The surface of the Moon is marked by millions of craters. These craters vary in size from a few yards across to hundreds of miles in diameter. Most of the craters formed a long time ago when comets, asteroids, and **meteorites** crashed onto the Moon's surface. You can explore how different craters are made and how soil is dug up in this activity.

1 Fill the pan about a ¾ inch deep with flour. Lightly sprinkle the hot cocoa mix to cover the entire surface of the flour. The chocolate and white flour act as the upper soil and deeper layers of the Moon.

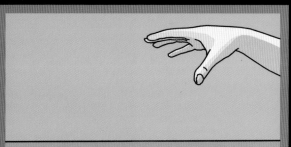

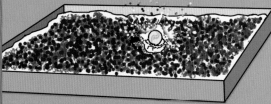

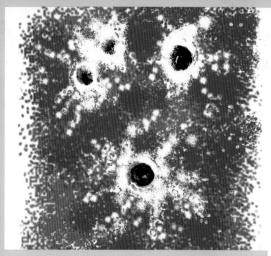

2 To make a model of the Moon's surface, drop (do not throw!) the marbles one at time into the pan. The marbles act as the crashing asteroids and comets.

3 Notice how the marbles make craters in the pan. The soil below the surface (flour) is brought to the surface. The Moon's biggest craters also reveal deeper layers of its crust.

Drop different sized marbles to see their impact. Drop marbles of the same size from different heights. Marbles dropped from the greatest height will make larger craters, because they have more energy.

WHAT'S IN A NAME?

Many of the Moon's craters have their own names. Some are named after scientists and artists including Albert Einstein, Leonardo da Vinci, and Alexander Fleming.

FULL MOON TO NO MOON

The shape of the Moon seems to change during the month. It is as though a giant monster keeps taking bites out of the Moon.

The Moon is not really changing its shape. What you see are the different parts of the Moon that are lit up by the light of the Sun falling on it. You see different parts of the Moon lit up depending on where the Moon is in its orbit around the Earth. The changing shapes are called the phases of the Moon.

3. First Quarter

4. Waxing Gibbous

27-DAY MOON CYCLE

5. Full Moon

6. Waning Gibbous

HARVEST MOON

An equinox is a time when day and night are equal in length. The full Moon closest to the autumn or fall equinox (usually around September 22 or 23) is called a harvest Moon. Traditionally this is when farmers brought in their crops before winter.

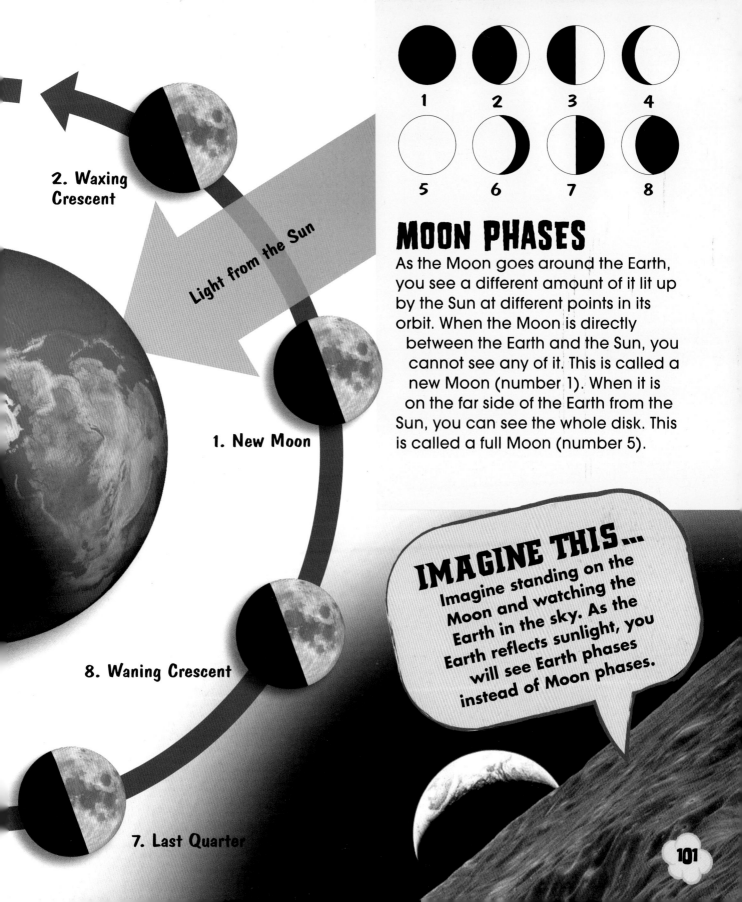

2. Waxing Crescent

Light from the Sun

1. New Moon

8. Waning Crescent

7. Last Quarter

1 2 3 4

5 6 7 8

MOON PHASES

As the Moon goes around the Earth, you see a different amount of it lit up by the Sun at different points in its orbit. When the Moon is directly between the Earth and the Sun, you cannot see any of it. This is called a new Moon (number 1). When it is on the far side of the Earth from the Sun, you can see the whole disk. This is called a full Moon (number 5).

IMAGINE THIS...

Imagine standing on the Moon and watching the Earth in the sky. As the Earth reflects sunlight, you will see Earth phases instead of Moon phases.

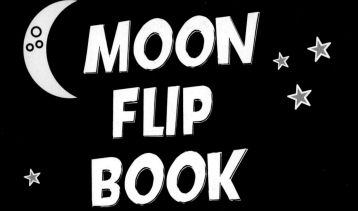

MOON FLIP BOOK

We have learned in this book that as the Moon circles the Earth, its shape appears to change slightly every night. This happens because different amounts of the sunlit part of the Moon are facing us on the Earth. In this activity, you can make a flip book of the Moon's different phases. These will cover the pattern of phases from new Moon to full Moon and back to new Moon.

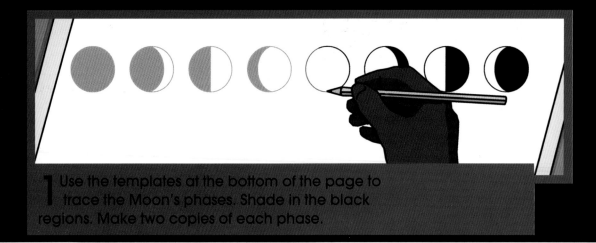

1 Use the templates at the bottom of the page to trace the Moon's phases. Shade in the black regions. Make two copies of each phase.

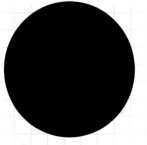
1. New Moon

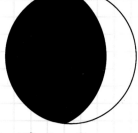
2. Waxing Crescent

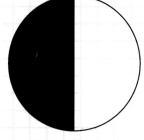
3. First Quarter

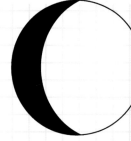
4. Waxing Gibbou

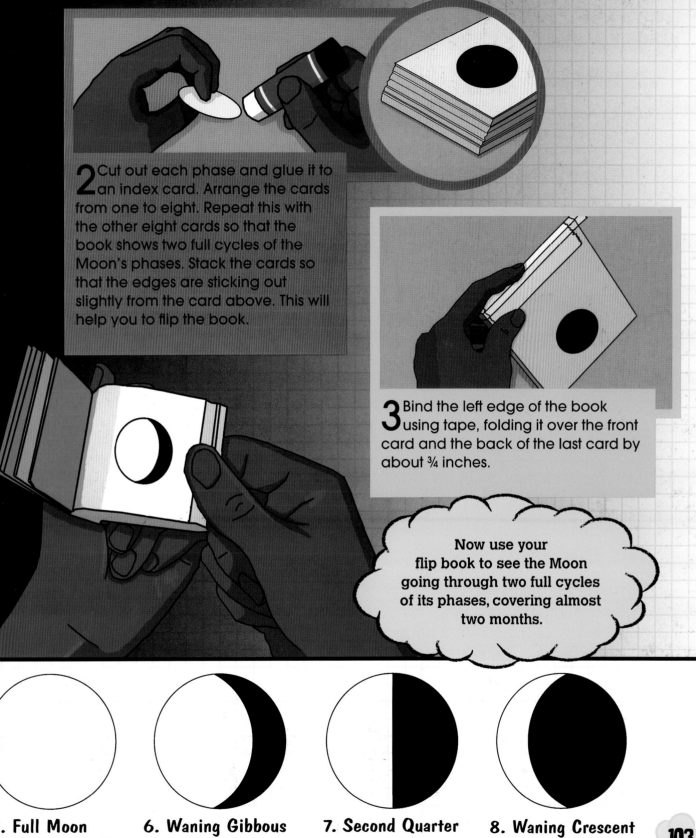

2 Cut out each phase and glue it to an index card. Arrange the cards from one to eight. Repeat this with the other eight cards so that the book shows two full cycles of the Moon's phases. Stack the cards so that the edges are sticking out slightly from the card above. This will help you to flip the book.

3 Bind the left edge of the book using tape, folding it over the front card and the back of the last card by about ¾ inches.

Now use your flip book to see the Moon going through two full cycles of its phases, covering almost two months.

. **Full Moon**   6. **Waning Gibbous**   7. **Second Quarter**   8. **Waning Crescent**

FROM DAY TO NIGHT

We all know that when the Sun is in the sky, it is daytime, and after the Sun sets, it gets dark. During the day, the Sun appears to move across the sky, rising in the east, and setting in the west.

But the Sun is not really moving around us! It appears to move because the Earth is spinning on its **axis** and taking us along with it. The time it takes for the Earth to rotate once fully is called a day. As it turns, people living on the part of the Earth facing the Sun experience day, and everyone on the part facing away from the Sun is in darkness. As the Earth continues to spin, the region of daylight moves across the globe from east to west.

MAKE YOUR DAY!

Use a globe to see how the spinning Earth leads to day and night. Mark where your city or country is on the globe with a sticker. Now shine the light of a flashlight onto the globe to act as sunlight. Slowly rotate the globe on its axis and see how the sticker moves into and out of the light from the flashlight, resulting in day and night. Note which countries are in darkness when it is daytime where you live.

EARTH AT NIGHT

During the hours of darkness, we use artificial lights to help us see. If you look at the Earth from a satellite in orbit, you can see the built-up areas in the half where it is nighttime lit up by streetlights.

IMAGINE THIS...

If the Earth rotated twice as quickly as it does, our days would be half as long. The weather would become much stormier, with much stronger winds.

A LONG DAY

All the planets spin on their axes. Some spin faster than the Earth, while others turn more slowly. This means that the lengths of the day and night are different on the other planets. Venus (right) takes 243 Earth days to turn. It takes just 225 Earth days to orbit the Sun, which means that a Venus day is longer than a Venus year!

A ZOO OF STARS

Look up at the clear night sky from a dark location, far away from city streetlights, and you may be able to see thousands of stars.

Stars appear as tiny dots in the sky because they are so distant. Look carefully and you will see that stars are not all the same color. Most appear white, but some have an orange, reddish, or blue color. Stars are also not all the same brightness; some shine more brilliantly than others. The night sky is full of many different types of star.

STAR BIRTH

Stars do not stay the same forever. They have a birth, life, and death. All stars are born in clouds of dust and gas. Gradually, gravity pulls the dust and gas together, and at the center of the cloud, a future star, called a protostar, starts to form.

RED GIANT

Our Sun will last for 10 billion years. It is currently about halfway through its life. Toward the end of its life, it will expand to become a red giant. It will swallow up Mercury, and the Earth will become so hot that its oceans will boil. But do not worry, it will not happen for a very long time yet.

WHITE DWARF

After swelling into a red giant, the Sun will throw off its outer layers to leave the hot core, and a shell of gas known as a planetary nebula (such as the Eskimo Nebula, right). Over the next few billion years, the core will cool and fade to become a white dwarf.

SUPERNOVA

Stars that are much heavier than the Sun have a more explosive end to their lives. These monster stars last only a few million years before they run out of energy to shine. The star dies in a spectacular explosion called a supernova.

IMAGINE THIS...

After a star has blown up in a supernova explosion, what is left behind is crushed into a tiny space until it forms a black hole. Nothing, not even light, can escape from a black hole.

107

CONSTELLATION IN YOUR HAND

People have been looking at the night sky for thousands of years—even before telescopes were invented. Many have seen pictures or patterns in the way certain stars are grouped together. These pictures are called constellations. Here are six constellations that you can hold in your hand and look at. After you have tried this activity, see if you can find the real constellations in the night sky.

YOU WILL NEED:

- six cardboard tubes
- aluminum foil
- six labels
- pencil
- tracing paper
- scissors
- tape
- thumbtack

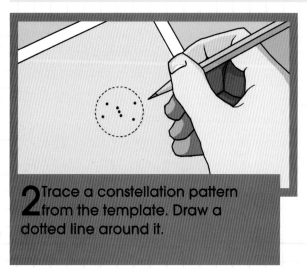

2 Trace a constellation pattern from the template. Draw a dotted line around it.

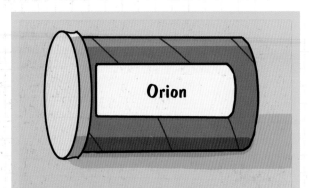

Orion

1 Take the cardboard tubes and cover one end with foil. Label each tube with a different constellation from the list on the right.

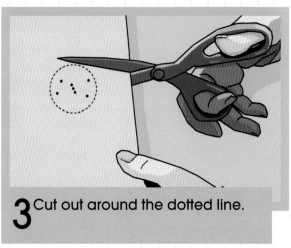

3 Cut out around the dotted line.

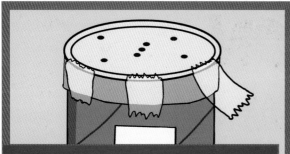

4 Place the pattern face-down on the foil on the tube with the matching label. You should still see the reversed pattern through the paper. Tape the pattern into place.

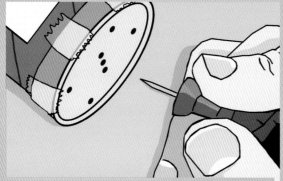

5 Using the thumbtack, punch a hole through the tracing paper and the foil for each star in the pattern.

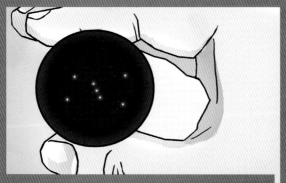

6 Remove the tracing paper. You should be able to hold the tube toward a light, look into the open end, and see the constellation as if you were looking into the night sky!

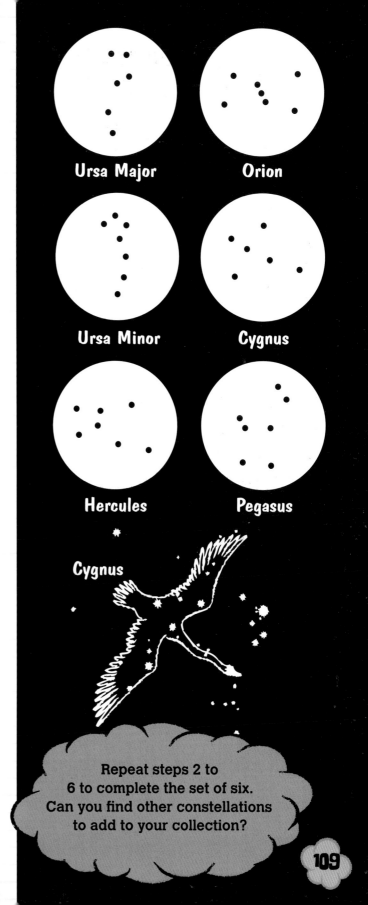

Ursa Major

Orion

Ursa Minor

Cygnus

Hercules

Pegasus

Cygnus

Repeat steps 2 to 6 to complete the set of six. Can you find other constellations to add to your collection?

NEW WORLDS FAR AWAY

One of the most amazing new discoveries in astronomy today is that our Sun is not the only star that has a system of planets orbiting it.

Using powerful telescopes on the Earth and in space, astronomers have so far found nearly 500 planets orbiting other stars far away. Planets going around other stars (and not the Sun) are called exoplanets.

IMAGINE THIS...

Maybe an exoplanet could have blue seas and white clouds. Or perhaps it has black plants. Maybe it has two moons. Draw some pictures showing how an exoplanet might look.

GOLDILOCKS PLANETS

The recent discovery of exoplanets has led to a hunt for rocky planets like the Earth that have living things on them. Think how fantastic it would be to know for sure that there was life, maybe like humans, on another planet very far away. Astronomers are looking for exoplanets that are the right distance from their star. Just like Goldilocks's porridge, the planet must not be too hot or too cold! It has to be just the right temperature so that oceans can exist on its surface. The presence of liquid water on a planet makes it more able to support life.

EARTHLIKE PLANETS

It is thought there may be millions more planets waiting to be discovered. Most of the exoplanets uncovered so far are giant gas planets like Jupiter and Saturn. It is very exciting to think that we might soon find an Earthlike planet orbiting a distant, Sunlike star!

Space telescope

TELESCOPES

Astronomers use powerful telescopes with mirrors that can be many yards across. Huge observatories are perched on mountains around the world, such as in Hawaii. Some telescopes are so high up that they sit above most of the Earth's clouds! There are also telescopes in space that orbit the Earth, such as the Hubble Space Telescope. They have huge solar panels that generate power by converting sunlight into electricity.

Observatory

A UNIVERSE OF GALAXIES

SPIRAL-SHAPED

The bright stars in our galaxy, the Milky Way, make a spiral-shaped structure, like a large, rotating pinwheel, in space. The galaxy is so large that light takes almost 100,000 years to travel from one side to the other.

Our Sun and its planets are just tiny specks among the 100 billion other stars that are held together by gravity to make our galaxy, which is called the Milky Way.

The universe itself is vast and contains all of the matter and energy we know of. The universe contains about 100 billion galaxies, which come in a variety of shapes and sizes. Our galaxy is a spiral galaxy.

A BIG BANG!

Astronomers believe that the universe began almost 14 billion years ago. They call the moment when the universe started the **big bang**. At first, the universe was an incredibly hot and tiny bubble. The energy released from the big bang made the universe grow. It might continue to expand forever, or it could stop growing and start to shrink back down into a tiny bubble.

10,000,000,000,000,000,000,000

ELLIPTICAL

These egg-shaped galaxies may have 1 trillion stars in them. While spiral galaxies have lots of old and new stars, elliptical galaxies have mostly old stars.

LENTICULAR

Between spiral galaxies and elliptical galaxies are the disk-shaped lenticular galaxies. Like ellipticals, they contain mainly very old stars.

IRREGULAR

Sometimes, a galaxy has no regular shape, perhaps because it crashed into another galaxy. Irregular galaxies have lots of new stars in them.

IMAGINE THIS...

Look up at the night sky and imagine how many stars there are. There are as many stars in the universe as there are grains of sand on all the Earth's beaches.

COLLIDING

Sometimes we can see two spiral galaxies colliding with each other. In time, these two colliding galaxies will combine to form one irregular galaxy.

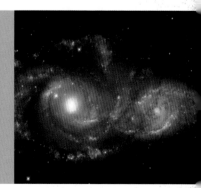

PAPER COMET

Comets are balls of snow, ice, dust, and rock. Sometimes a comet comes close to the Sun. It partially melts and a spectacular tail streams out behind it. Follow these steps to make a paper comet.

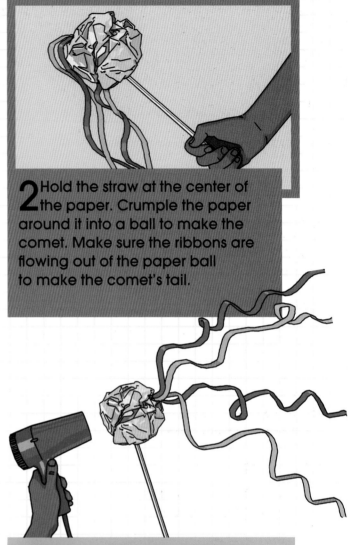

2 Hold the straw at the center of the paper. Crumple the paper around it into a ball to make the comet. Make sure the ribbons are flowing out of the paper ball to make the comet's tail.

3 Ask an adult to plug in the hairdryer. Blow air onto your comet to make the tails stream away. The air from the dryer is acting like the solar wind that flows from the Sun.

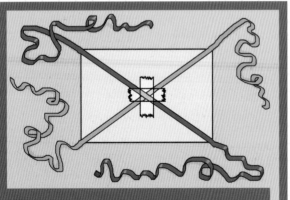

1 Lay down two ribbons across the sheet of paper to make an "X" shape. The ribbons should stretch at least a yard away from each corner. Put tape across the "X" where the ribbons cross.

Walk around the Sun (hairdryer) holding the comet, making sure the air is pointing at the comet. Notice how the tails always point away from the Sun.

GLOSSARY

ARTIFICIAL
Something that has been made by humans and does not occur naturally.

ASTEROID
A medium-sized rocky object that orbits the Sun.

ATMOSPHERE
The layer of gases that surrounds a planet or moon.

AXIS
An imaginary line around which a planet or moon spins.

BIG BANG
The idea that the Universe began with an explosive event.

BLACK HOLE
A region of space with such strong gravitational pull that nothing can escape it.

COMET
A small icy object made of gas and dust that orbits around the Sun.

CORROSIVE
A chemical that slowly destroys something else.

CRATER
A bowl-shaped hole made on planets or moons by objects crashing from space.

DISSOLVING
Breaking up into such small pieces that the pieces from one substance mix completely with another substance.

FILTERING
Separating two substances by passing them through a sieve.

FLEXIBLE
Something that will bend without breaking.

FORCE
Action on an object that causes its motion to change speed or direction. Gravity and friction are types of force.

FREEZE
When something cools so much that it turns from a liquid into a solid.

GALAXY
A collection of billions of stars, gas, and dust held together by gravity.

GALVANIZED
Coated with zinc.

GILLS
The parts of a fish that sit behind its head. They take oxygen out of the water so that the fish can breathe.

GRAVITY
A pulling force that attracts objects to each other.

GRID
A system for distributing electric power throughout a region.

LATERAL LINE
The sensitive line that runs along the side of a fish. It detects sounds and movements underwater.

LUNGS
Sponge-like body parts in the chest of many animals. They allow oxygen to pass into the body and carbon dioxide to pass out of it.

MELT
When something warms up so much that it turns from a solid into a liquid.

METEORITE
A rock-like object that lands on the Earth or on the Earth's Moon.

MOON
A small object that moves around a planet.

ORBIT
To move around an object in a specific path. It can also mean the path itself.

PLANET
A large, round object that moves around a star.

POLLINATION
When the male and female parts of a plant join together to create seeds.

PREDATOR
An animal that hunts other animals.

PRISM
A transparent object that breaks up light into the different colours of the rainbow.

PULSE
The regular beating made by your blood as your heart pushes it through your blood vessels.

RAW MATERIALS
Natural substances that can be used to make artificial chemicals and substances.

RECYCLE
To reuse something, either in the same state or changed to make something new.

SOLAR SYSTEM
The eight planets, many dwarf planets and other objects that orbit the Sun.

UNIVERSE
The whole of space, matter and energy, including all planets, stars and galaxies.

VIBRATING
Moving to and fro or up and down very quickly and repeatedly.

INDEX

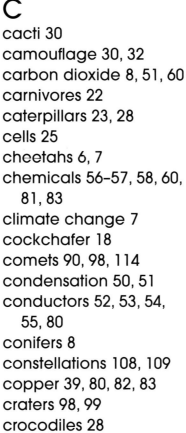

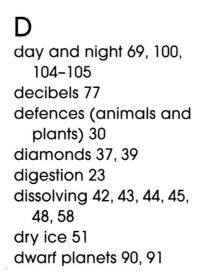

R

rainbows 72–73
ramps 62
raw materials 36
reactions (chemical) 56, 60
reactions (movements) 21
recycling 37
red giants 107
reflection 70, 71
reflexes 20
refraction 72, 73
reproduction 10, 28
reptiles 14, 18, 24
rocky planets 90, 94, 110
roots 8, 11, 13

S

salt 44, 45, 48
Saturn 90, 91, 94, 111
screws 62
seals 29
seaweeds 8
seeds 8, 10, 11, 12–13
senses 14–15
shadows 68, 69
shellfish 19, 30
sieving 43
silver 37, 80
simple machines 62–63
skyscrapers 36

snakes 14, 18
solar panels 93, 111
solar system 90, 91, 92, 96
solids 42, 46, 47
solutes 42
solutions 42, 48
solvents 42
sound 24, 74–77
sound waves 74, 76
spectrum 72
sponges 18
stars 88, 90, 92, 106–107, 112, 113
steam 50, 51, 80
steel 34, 36, 47, 84, 86
stone 35, 36
Sun 68, 90, 92–93, 101, 104, 107
sunlight 7, 8, 9, 13, 14, 68, 71, 101
sunspots 92
supernova 107
suspensions 42
swimming 19

T

teeth 22
telescopes 88, 111
temperatures 51
transparent substances 68
trees 7, 8, 9
turbines 80

U

ultrasound 77
universe 112
Uranus 90, 91, 94

V

vapour 45, 50
Venus 90, 91, 94, 105
vibration 24, 74, 75
vocal cords 75
voice box 24, 75
volcanoes 60, 96, 97
volts and voltages 81
volume 76, 77

W

water 46, 47, 48, 49, 71, 80, 90, 110
water pressure 38
wavelength 76
wedges 62
whales 25, 28, 29, 75
wheels 62, 63, 65
white dwarfs 107
white light 72, 73
wood 35, 36, 52, 80
wool 38, 39
worms 25

PICTURE CREDITS